WHAT PEOPLE ARE SAYING ABOUT *FULL S.T.E.A.M. AHEAD*

"Gayle's book illustrates the journey of similar women in S.T.E.A.M. who have made the brave choice to move onto the next phase of their life's path, some out of necessity and some out of choice. Through their stories and her wise guidance, there are lessons to be gleaned for women contemplating a similar set of options. For some it makes sense to stay in their corporate jobs, and use these learnings to better navigate the corporate ladder. In addition, Gayle's insights can serve corporate management teams who seek to retain their best people, and how to adopt and apply DEI best practices to support and empower the talented women they've worked so hard to recruit and train."

— Kelli Richards, President & Chief Connection Officer at The All Access Group LLC

"This book shows the importance of gender inclusivity when it comes to closing the gender gaps in the S.T.E.A.M. fields."

— Esther Wojcicki, Co-Founder of Tract.app and the "Godmother of Silicon Valley"

"The 'all-boys' club is no more! Gayle's book dives full S.T.E.A.M. ahead into the lives of successful women as they navigate each individual landscape on their way to full empowerment. Nothing comes easy and whether you're a man or a woman, this book will give you the tools to conquer every challenge & steamroll every obstacle in the workplace."

— Jeffrey Hayzlett, Primetime TV & Podcast Host, Speaker, Author, and Part-Time Cowboy

"Gayle 'gets it' and has a style that empowers others to learn and exude confidence."

— Lori Dempsey, Senior Business Applications
Sales Executive, Microsoft

"Challenges in the workplace abound - especially for women in S.T.E.A.M. careers. Gender bias is more subtle than it was when I started my career, but its hidden nature makes it more insidious. Don't be beat by it. *Full S.T.E.A.M. Ahead* offers actionable and transformative tools to cut through the obstacles and chart your course to empowerment and leadership."

— Janine Firpo, Author of *Activate Your Money* and
Co-Founder, Invest for Better

TRIUMPHANT TALES for Working Women to Overcome Adversity, Fear, and Self-Doubt

Full S.T.E.A.M. *Ahead*

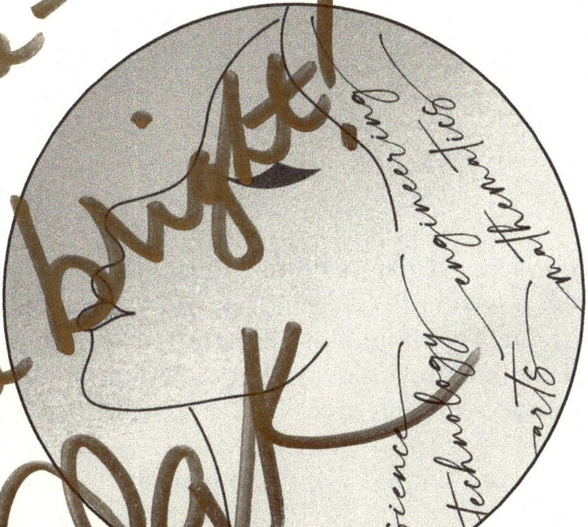

Yvonne—
Shine bright!
GK

gk GAYLE KELLER

Publishing support provided by
Ignite Press
5070 N. Sixth St. #189
Fresno, CA 93710
www.IgnitePress.us

ISBN: 979-8-9864279-0-4
ISBN: 979-8-9864279-1-1 (Hardcover)
ISBN: 979-8-9864279-2-8 (E-book)

For bulk purchase and for booking, contact:

Gayle Keller
Gayle@GayleKeller.org
https://www.GayleKeller.org

Library of Congress Control Number: 2022910792

Cover design by Anis El Idrissi
Edited by Elizabeth Arterberry
Interior design by Jetlaunch

FIRST EDITION

DEDICATION

This book is dedicated to the future leaders of this world: my beautiful daughters, Taylor and Avery, who inspire me every day with greater hope for our future. I love being your mother and love watching you confidently and courageously chase your dreams. Remember, I am always in your hearts.

To my husband, James: I'm incredibly grateful for your unwavering support and encouragement as I chase my dreams of leaving this world a more equitable place. Thank you for being my partner while we raise two incredibly strong, competent, intelligent, beautiful, fun, and charismatic girls.

To my nieces, Harper Wolski, Sloan Wolski, and Karsyn Keller, and my Goddaughters, Harper, Natalie Manfredini, and Tessa Trentacosti: may the work of my generation build a strong, empowering, and equitable platform for your generation, and may you always know your inner superpowers and follow your inner wisdom.

To my Godson and nephew, Grayson Keller: may you always continue to support, empower, and believe in the women and men who surround you, and be a leader who others want to follow.

To my brother, Ryon: Thank you for being my "little big brother." I'm forever grateful for the strong bond that we share where we both look out for each other and are each other's champions and confidantes. The world is a better place because your most powerful legacy is your beautiful family.

To my mother, Julie Wolski (a.k.a. Chief): You taught me how to laugh at myself, to have a sense of humor, and to always emulate kindness—as well as instilling in me a love of cooking. For Ryon and me, you taught and modeled living with a positive spirit and always finding the small positive in a negative situation, because that positive will get us through it, guiding us to recreate ourselves into even stronger people than we could have imagined. Thank you for always believing in me and loving me unconditionally. I love you forever.

To my late father, Edward Wolski: You instilled within me a great work ethic and showed me what it means to live and model an inclusive community and world. Your gift of unmatched wit made it easy for everyone to genuinely feel welcome in your presence. Your "Great Wolski Pour" certainly contributed to every ounce of fun you shared each and every time. If you were ever on the receiving end of my dad's limitless gift of hospitality, you know what I mean. You earned your wings on Christmas Eve 2021. Dad, please continue to send signs of encouragement and guidance as you watch over us. I love you forever.

ACKNOWLEDGMENTS

I also would like to acknowledge those who have been in my life, supported me, and encouraged me to pursue my dreams, as well as to stand up and speak out when necessary.

To my late grandfather, Theodore, who taught me anything is possible if I put my mind and elbow grease into it. I have his antique radio which inspired this book and my podcast series, Theodora Speaks™, as I liken podcasts to radio. I carry his entrepreneurial spirit and craving for good tasting rye bread, Polish sausage, and horseradish, and a guilty pleasure of collecting stylish shoes.

To my late "Aunt Marion" Lawson Hunter and Mrs. Elaine Love: Your confidence and courage were contagious. Thank you for instilling survival traits in me to last a lifetime.

To my sisters-in-law, Lindsey Wolski and Karolina Keller: Keep up the great work. You are wonderful mothers and aunts.

To the sister I never had whom I love dearly, my soul sister and cousin, Dr. Lisa Manfredini: Thank you for being a guiding light in my life. You are someone I admire and treasure. A martini and oysters always taste better in your presence.

To my beautifully talented and loving Confirmation sponsor and dear friend, Joan Bufalino: Thank you for always believing in me. I have never stopped looking up to you.

To my cousin Mary Koziol: from playing Barbies and riding bikes as kids to raising children of our own, life (and Kool-Aid!) is sweeter with you!

To *the* greatest networker I know, Curtis R. Simic: your friendship and mentorship are some of the greatest gifts I received during my collegiate experience at Indiana University.

To my kindred spirits and dear friends: your friendship has blessed me in helping me become a more confident, courageous, and braver person. You all are such incredibly strong, beautiful, and talented women.

- Lindsey Seavert Harrison
- Amy Dryer
- Adrienne Trentacosti
- Amy Stevens
- Beth Swierk
- Lara Massouras
- Lisa Doherty
- Abbie Mota
- Adrienne Williams LaBorwit
- Claire Sayers
- Cheryl Maletich
- Erin Slone
- Jill Martay
- Tricia Winterich
- Kristen Eder
- Michelle Harkin
- Amy Gillard
- Lea Dan
- Donna Kowalik
- Abby Main

To my smart mentors, Mary Powaga Anderson, Romi Mahajan, and James Wang, who saw something in me and said "yes" when I asked them to be my mentor.

To my valued business sponsors, Mark Everix, Kate Johnson, Rob Nehrbas III, and Jeff Jaeger: thank you for challenging me at every turn and for speaking positively on my behalf.

To my incredible business coach, Kelli Richards, who sees brilliantly around corners and is a strategic visionary where technology and media intersect.

To my irreplaceable managers, Craig Mandel, Sateen Manik, and John Siefert, who took a risk on hiring me. I learned a great deal and grew taller under your guidance.

To my favorite graduate professor, Candy Lee: You made education fun and memorable. You gave me the courage and sharpened my skills to take my leap of faith.

To my Theodora Speaks podcast guests: thank you all for sharing your inspiring and empowering stories that positively impact the world and aid in closing the gender gap in the S.T.E.A.M. fields.

And a special thank you to my fabulously talented book strategist, editor, and new friend, Cindy Tschosik.

Thank you all for believing in me. If it were not for all of you, I would not be the woman that I am today.

TABLE OF CONTENTS

FOREWORD

Curtis R. Simic, President Emeritus of the Indiana University Foundation

Gayle Wolski Keller has amazing skills of observation, perception, and analysis that began to emerge when I met her as a student at Indiana University. She headed a 300-member student organization that created and executed plans for major events to raise money for working student scholarships. Today, and in the book, her apparent values continue to be respect for others, empathy, a habit of listening in a very focused way, and the ability to recognize subtle nuances. As a leader, it's important to identify points of tension, even friction, to identify areas requiring improvement and enable her to formulate strategies to move matters and people towards optimum solutions. While attending Indiana, she was always respectful of herself and others because she knew then and knows now that all progress is built on mutual trust and clear, unambiguous conversation.

Recognizing today's cultural issues and the disparity of outcomes and opportunities for women that still persist in today's workplace, Keller was inspired to write this book to help women deal with the challenges they face in the workplace, including workplace bullying, sexual harassment, competition with fellow colleagues, lack of confidence, and mental health issues.

In doing so, she has added an important chapter to open the dialogue even more and support the quest to level the playing field as women pursue successful and satisfying careers in S.T.E.A.M. The playing field must be leveled. The stories of "The Five Theodoras" depict everyday women from five different cultures in the five different areas of S.T.E.A.M. who face, unfortunately, five common situations in today's society. As each life and challenge unfolds, Keller provides strategies and directions that can help women reach their full potential while adding value to the enterprises in which they are working. Following along with them and their experiences personalizes the deep bruises, being held back, or even being pushed aside and how they are propelled to overcome them, rise above, and ultimately succeed.

Thoreau wrote, "Go confidently in the direction of your dreams. Live the life you imagined." Those are empowering words, indeed, but there is not a single set of directions that is a fit for every woman. The five different journeys can be drawn upon, not exclusively or separately, but selectively to find which aspects come together to provide the unique plan for a single person.

Gayle's insights reflect her values—as do the works of all effective leaders. She is sensitive to the needs of others and seeks to apply the knowledge she gained at Microsoft, Indiana University, and Northwestern University by presenting these compelling stories of the five Theodoras. Their paths to elevating their careers are clearly expressed and illustrated through the construction of a substantive, practical storyline that creates a sense of progress and momentum.

This book adds a marvelous chapter to the efforts made across the globe by people and organizations intent on enabling women to embark on careers with every expectation of being appreciated, recognized, and compensated for their contributions. The resulting greater diversity and inclusion are essentials to improving the human condition.

INTRODUCTION

I was not always outgoing. In grade school, I struggled because I was not popular. Girls were mean and, therefore, I became known as "the mute." I was afraid to speak out because of fear and the judgment from others. It wasn't until high school that I blossomed into myself and found my voice through the speech team at Glenbard West High School in Illinois.

Known as "The Castle on the Hill," the campus has a magical, untouchable austerity. Perhaps this is due to its famous alumni—such as actors Sean Hayes, Amy Carlson, and Gary Sinise—or maybe it's because it was used as the setting for the film *Lucas* (1986). (Watch for the football field and the lockers!)

In front of those infamous lockers is where we practiced our speeches and scripts. It's where I gained the confidence to be myself, to be 100%, authentically me. Participating on the speech team gave me the perseverance to hone in on life-long beneficial communications skills that I still tap into today. Then, in college, I discovered my leadership traits when I became the Vice President of the Indiana University Student Foundation (IUSF) under the direction of the greatest networker and mentor I know, Curtis R. Simic, President Emeritus of the Indiana University Foundation. Mr. Simic instilled the value of philanthropy in me and has become a good friend and mentor.

Both the speech team and IUSF gave me my wings to fly, and my courage gave me the confidence to love my unique traits and set them free. Now that I am a mother to two girls, my wishes for my beauties are for them to remain curious, laugh at themselves, have fun, never lose their voice in fear of judgment, be resilient, stand up for what they believe in, "find the beauty in the ashes," be respected and respectful, love their unique traits, and that I can give them the character-building tools that will empower them to soar and leave a positive mark on this world that makes their hearts sing.

As my journey through childhood, adulthood, and motherhood have melded over the years, this book was birthed out of my experience as a woman in tech, as a woman in S.T.E.A.M. (Science, Technology, Engineering, Arts, and Mathematics), and as a participant in the continuous uphill battle women have to weather to thrive in male-dominated industries and workplaces.

Through my firsthand experiences as a WiSTEAM (woman in S.T.E.A.M.), I sought the best path forward to overcome obstacles in my way and turn those challenges into opportunities while staying engaged, asking questions, and being a good listener. When I began my career over twenty years ago, my work ethic, determination, and drive empowered me to learn, grow, and travel the world, submerging myself in other cultures. These experiences made me curious about empowering other women to follow their career aspirations while overcoming challenging situations they encounter in the workplace.

My wish is for this book to give a voice to the women who struggle with indecision, and that those women see their unique characteristics as game-changing superpowers that will aid them in taking calculated risks in their careers to elevate, expand, and/or reinvent their professional lives.

In this day and age, we are great at pointing fingers at others when something is not working to our advantage and rarely look in the mirror to see how we can improve upon ourselves. This book provides situations and models for how we can address issues head on while remaining appreciated and respected.

When it comes to reinventing my professional life and taking calculated risks, both personally and professionally, I've reflected on, analyzed, and assessed the processes and practices I've followed to formulate a methodology that will lead other women to build the life and career of their dreams. In my presentations and workplace training, I teach calculated risk-taking based on the five traits that I myself practice to elevate, expand, and empower my career.

1. Decisiveness
2. Courage
3. Clarity
4. Confidence
5. Balance

Personally, I've learned that my superpower is #2, Courage. If I was not courageous, I would not be where I am today. The women depicted in this book illuminate the common issues women face in the workplace such as lack of confidence, work and family conflicts, competition from fellow colleagues, workplace bullying, sexual harassment, and mental health issues.

Each Theodora

- Is named "Theodora" (after my grandfather, Theodore, whose work ethic, love of travel, and style I admired; he helped shape me into the woman I am today), who I define as representing all women who are strong, intelligent, and successful in predominantly male S.T.E.A.M. careers.

- Is from a diverse background and each is a different ethnicity.
- Earned her professional position in a specific S.T.E.A.M. industry.
- Shares her story.
- Faces her own workplace challenge, which is based upon one of the most common issues women in S.T.E.A.M. face today.
- Takes a cold, hard look at herself and asks herself how she can improve her self-worth.
- Examines her surroundings, current state of being, and dreams about her future while taking control of the brushstrokes to paint her own portrait.
- Demonstrates how they rely on their support system and how they look within to assess their goals, needs, and wants.
- Develops a plan to overcome their particular professional hurdle that could otherwise have a devastating impact on their careers and lives.

Each chapter offers a blueprint and lessons on how to improve oneself in and each of the depicted scenarios.

I'm honored to introduce you to the Five Theodoras, who have defined their key pillar, superpower, and profession, which has led them to their desired success.

- Silla™ believes "Clarity" empowered her to be sensational in Science.
- Tyriqa™ believes "Decisiveness" empowered her to be tenacious in Technology.
- Elaine™ believes "Confidence" empowered her to be exquisite in Engineering.
- Antonia™ believes "Courage" empowered her to be assertive in Arts.
- Maalika™ believes "Balance" empowered her to be motivated in Mathematics.

As you read, study, and hopefully embody each Theodora, I hope you recognize yourself within them, explore your future, and find solutions that will work for situations you encounter in your profession. Enjoy meeting them at each turn of the chapter.

Cheers to your inner Theodora,

Gayle Keller

PILLAR 1: CLARITY

SILLA, THE SENSATIONAL SCIENTIST

Silla cranked up the music to the highest volume as the car roof retracted. She called upon Bruno Mars once again to put her in her "Happy" state.

"Dammit. When will they listen to me? I am so tired of trying to oversell my ideas, only for them to be dismissed by these men!" Silla pressed the gas pedal to the floor of her pebble gray BMW convertible.

As an introvert, it took a lot out of her to express anger, but occasionally, she needed to let out the steam. At times like this, she was grateful she picked a modest and unassuming convertible, where she could let out a little of her wild side that she didn't dream of exposing at work or in her personal social life.

It was the price she paid for growing up in her generation as an Asian American woman with the hefty price tag of being recognized as "sensational" in the science community. Silla had enjoyed science since she was three years old, and she came to appreciate math when she was just a bit older. Both subjects came naturally to her, but she was more drawn to the curiosity, surety, and clarity that science offered, when solutions are birthed from the very theory expounded by the individual scientist or the team of scientists.

Thank God it's Friday, she thought. *This is going to take me a couple of days to get over, and I need to think through why this keeps happening.*

Her phone rings.

"Jenna!" *It's so good to hear a friendly voice.* "Yes! I'm excited about our cooking lesson tomorrow… I love curry. Yes, 6:30 is great for pickup. I'll be ready." She pressed the end button and inhaled a big breath and exhaled a full cleansing breath.

"My day is looking up. At least I have something to look forward to." She cranked the music up louder as "Love Myself" by Hailee Steinfield filled the airwaves. "Ah yes, the universe is lifting me up!"

As one hand stayed on the wheel, she pumped her free hand into the air and yelled out a healing scream, releasing all her frustration. The kids from the neighborhood looked at her peculiarly as she pulled into her driveway.

"Hey, Miss Silla!" Little eight-year-old Ava waved.

Ava was a doll, always helping the neighbors with their gardens—a true green thumb. Silla reminded herself that the frustrations she had dealt with for the last ten years would not exist when Ava was in the working world—at least, that was her hope. She walked through the front door, put her keys in the tray on the foyer table, and dropped her bag near the coat closet door. "Home Sweet Home."

At the bottom of the stairs, she slipped off her size six DIOR sneakers right next to her Jimmy Choo Bing Crystal shoes, walked to the fridge, and grabbed a bottle of Perrier.

"Alexa, play Tata Young."

The smooth beats filled the room and kept her from replaying every word that was uttered, every attempt she made to be heard only to be abruptly cut off by every man in the lab.

"That's my dolly, Mrs. Rossi. Her name is Elizabeth. Isn't her long red hair beautiful?" Silla heard Ava's young, shrill voice through the closed window in the kitchen.

As Silla poured her sparkling water into a crystal wine glass, her own aspirations as a little girl flooded her mind. She had known she would want to be a scientist from a very young age. While other kids played with dolls, Silla always secretly wanted to blow something up. In third grade, she had welcomed her first individual science experiment.

Silla sat down and tucked her legs under her, took a long sip, and threw her head back against the velvety soft couch cushion, shutting her eyes as she recalled her prized pink volcano that spewed fuchsia lava. People had laughed during her demonstration at the open house, but Silla, being the strong, steadfast, determined future scientist she was, didn't care about what other people thought. Her eyes were set on that bright blue ribbon. Instead, David proudly gloated about his first place award while she claimed third place.

"Well, at least I placed," she said out loud to the empty gathering room. Even all this time later, she questioned the judges' first-place pick of an ant farm. Although she had still been recognized, winning third place, self-doubt had settled in. Would she ever really be the scientist she was born to become?

How could hope and self-doubt coexist in the same brain at the same time?

For twenty years, Silla advanced her exemplary skills and talents in the unique field of epidemiology, the study of predicting, classifying, and controlling unique diseases. She worked alongside mad scientists, disheveled geniuses, and perfectionists. She considered herself to be a nice blend of the latter two, minus the disheveled. She was more methodical than mad, and liked everything neat, simple, and to have clarity and purpose—just like her favorite social drink, a lychee tequila shooter. The delicate, sophisticated drink brought pleasure to the eyes with its light pink, translucent shimmer, while its smooth texture and pronounced flavor awakened all the senses at the prime point of indelible pleasure. It was a luxury she only enjoyed in the company of her closest girlfriends. She shied away from social outings at work because they were awkward, especially in a male-dominated field.

Her therapist had advised her, "Silla, work social events are important because that is where coworking relationships are built, where people learn to trust you and get to know you."

"I guess I could go out for a glass of chardonnay after my yoga and mindful breathing class one of these days," she sheepishly agreed.

It was funny, the stereotypes people had about each other in the workplace. At first glance, Silla could easily be categorized as a perfectionist, with her straight, brown, shoulder-length bob that was smooth as silk and without a stray hair to be seen. But she found perfectionism too stifling and lacking in flexibility and creativity, traits she needed in order to explore and expand as she developed intimate knowledge of the complexities of viruses, illnesses, and diseases. There were so many factors to consider in her work to discover the best pathway to cures and wellness in humans. She firmly believed that nothing was ever off the table. Which was one of the reasons, she believed, that she bumped heads so much with colleagues. This had caused self-doubt to settle into her soul, suppressing her confidence and leading her to become obsessed with the thought, "Am I even good enough?"

"Ugh! Imposter syndrome! Why do I have to deal with this every day?" She's worked on it, among many other skills, in her weekly conversations with her therapist. "Oh, to be eight again. Lucky Ava!

"Okay! Enough of a pity party, Silla! Get yourself together. You are an accomplished and recognized scientist. Your whole life goal is to become known as 'Silla, the sensational scientist,' and that takes years. Yes, sure, growing up, a lot of women did not become scientists, so what! You were raised to believe that 'if you see it, you can achieve it.' So, perhaps women have not risen side-by-side with the men who are climbing the ranks in this field, but it just takes one person with perseverance, tenacity, and the drive to achieve her dreams. And *you*, Silla, have all of that and more."

Her eyes opened to the cobalt blue and silver chandelier above her.

"Oh my gosh! It's dark. Ouch. There's a crick in my neck. How long have I been sitting here like this? I'm starving," she said to herself as she stood up, stretched, picked up her wine glass and headed to the kitchen.

In the pantry, she found ramen noodles. In the fridge was the leftover sushi from dinner out with her best friend, Mandy. "I guess it's salmon nigiri and ramen. Oh, there's some lemon broccoli from last night. All the food groups. Mom would be proud."

As she opened the container of ramen, a memory flooded her senses. She often made pho from scratch with her mom in the kitchen when she was younger. Cooking in that kitchen brought with it a sense of security and a rush of warmth, one that ran through Silla's entire body. She was reminded of how her mom emphasized that the art of cooking was a trifecta—a sprinkle of science, a dash of art, and a pinch of love.

"Oh, Mom, I wish I could make homemade pho noodles with you right now," she said aloud.

The cat, Allis, meowed. "Shoot! I need to feed you. Allis, I'm so sorry."

She finished dinner and washed the dishes. *Don't put off tomorrow what can be done today*, her dad's voice played in her head. It was true; she was neat and tidy in every possible way. Even the cat picked up the neatness of the house after living at the humane society for seven months.

Heading to her bedroom, she paused at the stairway, bent over and picked up both pairs of shoes. "Ahhh. Someday, I'll build my Sarah Jessica Parker shoe closet. Wouldn't it be cool to have it on the first floor? Who puts their shoes on in their bedroom anyway? I surely don't."

Shoes, it was funny to have that as the one splurge she afforded herself for hard work. And how people noticed shoes, of all things! Instead of, "I love your dress" or "You have a nice smile," people immediately loved her shoes. It was the ultimate icebreaker, especially as she sometimes found it nerve-wracking to talk to people or to be the first one to start a conversation. When she was younger, her mom coached her on how to make friends by making direct eye contact and small talk. With a great disdain for small talk, she played the script in her head over a thousand times before going anywhere. "Hi. My name is Silla. I really like your shoes. What's your name? Where are you from? Do you have any brothers or sisters? What is your favorite food?"

Perhaps that's why she was so attracted to shoes. It was the spark that someone else lit to start a conversation with her, the exact way she wanted it.

Now in her bathroom, Silla walked to her soaking tub, turned it on, adjusted the temperature, and added some Epsom bath salts scented in lavender and rosemary. It was a new self-care Friday night ritual for her to take a wonderful, calming, and rejuvenating bath, followed by reading a couple of chapters of a book. She always started a new book on Friday, and tonight, she looked forward to reading *From Tokyo with Love* by Sarah Kuhn. It was the next book in line on her shelf after *Ripping off the Hoodie* by Shannon Wilkinson, which she finished on Wednesday. She had lined her next three books up in order in her library. The fiction books stood on the shelf below what she called her "professional bookshelf," which housed one of her favorite books on the art of storytelling, *Slide:ology* by Nancy Duarte.

Ahhh. Friday night soaks symbolized the soaking up of the week's accomplishments and the washing away of the week's challenges. Only weddings, funerals, and now, viruses were allowed to interrupt her Friday night schedule; otherwise, it was "Silla's Sensational Sunset Soak"—even if the sun had already set.

After the week's and the day's challenges swirled down the drain, she committed Saturday to self-assessing, analyzing, and forming an action plan to overcome these ridiculous obstacles that she would no longer tolerate.

"I'm better than this," she proclaimed as she dried herself off with the combo terry cloth and seersucker bath sheet.

To avoid turning Saturday into an emotional roller coaster, she vowed to herself that she would approach the rigor methodically, as if she was performing a science experiment. Clarity. Simplicity. Sincerity. Authenticity. It was her code of honor to herself and her work. Science didn't have room for emotions or blurred lines. There was only one instance where you would be forgiven for expressing emotion, and that was only when you cured a disease. Then, and only then, could you celebrate, because people's lives would be saved.

"Oomph!" Silla woke with a start, opening her eyes to find Allis standing on her chest, staring her down. She was not happy.

"Oh, no! It's 9:30! You've missed your milk time. You know, Allis, you don't have to be so timely! I'm going to start calling you 'Big Ben,'" she chided, referring to the great bell clock in the Palace of Westminster. Out of bed, she grabbed her favorite lounge pants, tee-shirt, and scrunchie, threw them on, and headed to the kitchen.

As she warmed up the milk for Allis, the orange tabby purred and rubbed up against her leg. It was one of the many joys of having a cat, even if she was a bit bossy. Saturdays were their "connection" day, especially in the morning. As Allis lapped at her warmed milk and Silla sipped on her green smoothie, they cuddled, watched the birds, and skimmed the online news in the quiet of morning. Fully immersing oneself in the local and daily news was depressing, so Silla only read news and articles related to her work and field.

The media was still ripe with pandemic news, despite it being a few years after the COVID-19 virus initially flattened the world. Never before seen by any living human was a pandemic the size of the Coronavirus, and now, news reporters informed the public of the constant barrage of new virus strains. While she knew more than the media, it was important that she keep up on new changes or developments in the public's perception and understanding of the virus and its treatment options. At some point, she hoped they would begin to believe the experts being interviewed, the professional health organizations, and their own doctors instead of the pretty face on the camera, spewing assumptions that lacked any basis in fact.

When COVID-19 erupted in the United States, Friday night baths halted, as well as calm Saturday mornings with Allis. Silla worked around the clock, sleeping for 80-90 minute stints between researching notes and articles and medical journals on the subject of previous epidemics of the 1900s and 1800s. What an extraordinary time to be an epidemiologist. The pandemic, which was not yet over, only increased her love for science, her field, and her passion for public health.

The first year was the most challenging time in her life. The work needed only called upon the brightest and best scientists to determine the best solution and press forward with it. Once the vaccines had been distributed and administered, shifts became more standardized and more evenly distributed amongst the entire company. Every day, they witnessed, compiled, and reported the number of the most recent deaths. It was crushing to the mind, body, and spirit. Every time a report came in, it felt as if she was living outside of herself. It seemed like nothing she was doing mattered.

And then, it did. The work she did with her colleagues made a difference in so many lives. Seeing the number of deaths per week decrease and hospital ICUs emptying as the patients became well enough to go home made her feel that she'd truly made a difference during the height of the chaos and tragedy of the pandemic. In fact, she was the recipient of two Prizes for Scientific Breakthroughs for her contribution to identifying it as a virus and for exploratory research to design the vaccines.

When it was all said and done, she had been surrounded by so much death, and yet, she had truly seen so much hope in human beings all over the world as well, who banded together to help one another... from afar... with masks on. It was a lot, though.

Over the past year, after returning to a more "normal" schedule, she took stock of her life to determine how she could design her best life. She started by making a handy-dandy checklist.

- Career
- Family
- Friends
- Healthy Foods
- Exercise
- Companion
- Self-Care

She took one look at the list and rearranged it. After a pandemic, the world realized there were more essential elements to life than just work. *My work is important to the world, but it cannot be my be-all and end-all. I don't want to die in a lab.*

- Self-Care
- Healthy Foods
- Exercise
- Companion
- Family
- Friends
- Career

"Career is last?" Silla asked herself incredulously. *My whole life has been my career!*

She talked herself through how and why she had organized her checklist this way. The fact of the matter was that the pandemic opened eyes, minds, and souls. It drastically shifted the human population by number and by heart and spirit. People recognized how short life was and reset their priorities, and Silla felt the same pull. In order to achieve "Sensational Scientist" status, she needed to take care of herself first. The irony was that, with her prioritizing her health, self-care, and restful time, her contribution to work had increased dramatically and was getting noticed. It begged the question, "How do we do more when we are doing less?"

There has to be a book about that, she thought.

Finding family and friends above career was not as surprising as seeing that she had ranked "companion" above family and friends. *Hmmm.* She reflected on that revelation. *Companion? A mate? What, when, who? That would be nice... in the future.*

On one of her few days off from vaccine development, Silla shopped with her mom in a quaint downtown area of her city. They came across an animal shelter, and they wandered in there. Who doesn't love to pet a dog every now and again? She knew she was safe because she wasn't equipped to have a dog in her life. The poor thing would be alone all day.

She gave her love to every dog in every crate. With her heart hurting a little bit, she turned towards the corner of the shelter, and stopped short as an orange blur flew towards her face. Silla flinched to catch whatever it was and let out a brief scream. Her arms stretched out to catch the object and she immediately hugged the orange blur to her chest. When the commotion stopped, in her arms lay an orange tabby cat with the greenest, most soulful eyes she had ever seen. The cat gazed up at Silla. As they locked eyes, Silla's heart melted. The kitty purred.

The employee who had nearly knocked down Silla while chasing the cat profusely apologized. He had just been bringing her back from her bath, which she hated; plus, she was hungry. A finicky cat by nature (or species, really), she liked her meals served warm and on time. Silla's heart and head collided and fought with each other.

This wasn't supposed to happen. I didn't know they had cats here. I was just here to see the dogs.

Letting out an exasperated breath, she replied, "That's okay. Would you mind if we visit for a little while?"

The words were out of her mouth before she knew she was saying them.

"Oh, Silla!" her mom exclaimed. "Cats make wonderful companions for working women!"

"Companion? What?" Silla questioned as she recalled her "Best Life Checklist."

The employee nodded. "That would be wonderful. I need to warm her food, and I could really use the distraction."

He led Silla, her mom, and the kitty to a little gated room and left abruptly to get the "Queen" her on-demand meal. When they were all settled, the kitty walked between Silla and her mom to get a sense of the two of them. She did this weird thing, though. She walked backwards every time she finished walking in a circle. It was charming and puzzling at the same time. The manager came by and explained it was just her particular way of communicating, although they hadn't figured out what she was saying, yet.

Ninety minutes later they were out the door with the kitty, a litter box, food, and all the fixings for a first-time pet owner.

It was love at first sight, and the kitty had not left Silla's side the entire time, except to walk backward towards Silla's mom.

Once they had buckled into their seat belts, her mom asked, "What are you going to name her?"

"Something to do with 'backwards.' I love that quirk of hers."

Mom clapped excitedly. "I know! How about your name spelled backwards?"

"A-L-L-I-S… Mom, that's perfect! Allis, here, kitty kitty."

Safe in her crate, Allis purred her approval.

Full and armed with the day's news, Silla let out a deep, cleansing breath. It was better to breathe than get annoyed, upset, and angry about the misinformation the public received.

"Well, there are bigger problems today. Allis, we need to get down to business."

Perrier in one hand and an apple in the other, Silla marched to her home office with Allis trotting behind her. The cat seemed to sense her owner was in for the day as she watched Silla grab the black, dark gray, and light gray dry-erase markers and walk to her whiteboard wall.

Silla pointed the gray marker at Allis. "It's all business today, Allis. We are figuring this out once and for all."

The cat looked up at her, bored, licked her paw three times, curled herself up in a ball, and peered over her furry self as she settled in for her morning nap.

"Okay, we are going to start with petri dishes. Why? Because there is something awful about how I think and behave that is contradictory to who I am and what I am capable of."

Instead of ruminating on Friday's debacle, Silla decided to map it out, much like she did when approaching the results of tests run at work and how they fit with her hypotheses. She would approach her problem one step at a time, in a digestible format with attainable goals. The answers were in front of her; she simply needed to list out the *who, what, why, when, where,* and *how* of this formula.

Though these were human beings she was considering, not viruses, there were some similarities between the two. For example, her growing displeasure that she was continuing to be talked over, dismissed, and disrespected by this same group of men every day of the week at work lingered like a bad flu. While she never would toot her own horn, she knew she was smarter than a lot of them, and clearly capable of her role. She knew her job would never be in jeopardy. She couldn't figure out whether her colleagues were acting this way because of her, personally, bad generational behavior, gender bias, or possibly even racial bias. Perhaps they did not even know their own rudeness because they assumed the way they treated her contributions was normal and acceptable.

It was a risk to lay it all out on her whiteboard—the good, the bad, and the ugly—but she couldn't continue like this. She had spent four years in therapy, and felt it was time to put everything she learned to good use.

She knew the solution to her problem lay within her, as well as within her workplace's culture, the behavior of her co-workers, and the company as a collective. Overcoming these obstacles would help her peel away yet another layer to reveal her best self. But the scared birdie in her soul was simultaneously fluttering and petrified, almost as if trapped in a cage. The bird symbolized her nervousness and shyness. Something had to change. Some*one* had to change. But that change would have to start with her.

She drew five circles resembling petri dishes on the board and identified the five areas to examine. One at a time. Step by step. Just like she set her 30/60/90 day goals and her five- and ten-year work plans.

"Silla, break it down into a digestible format, or you will be overwhelmed. You can't take on the whole enchilada in one bite," she encouraged herself. She gulped, grateful it was only Saturday, and she still had Sunday to recharge. Little by little, the issues took shape. She started with her ultimate goals.

"Me. Yes, let's start there." *I know me.*

She tapped the marker on the table in front of the board. "Well, I'm introverted. Always have been. Okay, Sensational Scientist, bring on the lists!"

Silla stepped back, grabbed her Perrier, and took a long drink out of the bottle. "Phew. That was not easy; it was much harder to write it on the board than it was to verbalize it to my therapist. Sheesh. You can never go wrong with honesty, so let's keep going.

"Well. That was truthful, tactful, and respectful. It could have gone a whole different direction if I was still ramped up from Friday. Emotions always kill productivity. I'm proud of myself for keeping it real without going off the rails."

Silla's Friday really sucked, though. It all went down in the lab. The all-male—aside from three women—research team was very well aware of her intense belief that there was an element or something missing in their approach to vaccine development. The current variant behaved similarly to a project she worked on in Africa, and she knew that, with one tweak, it could combat all of the strains of COVID and provide the essentials for a safe vaccine that could see long-term use against other variants.

"I know they are sick of me standing on my soapbox. I get it. But the fact of the matter is that we did it before, less than 100 years ago with the vaccines for measles, mumps, rubella, polio, and more. It's not unheard of, and I know I am on to something."

The answer was there. "Once I figure it out, I'll assemble focus groups, and have the group receiving the placebo and the group receiving the real vaccine report their ailments, feelings, emotions so we will have proof regarding its efficacy. All I know is I don't want to wear a mask the rest of my life!

"Wouldn't that be nice? It could even be true," Silla giggled at the last musing.

Every leader in her field that she contacted agreed that she was onto something and cheered her on. "Why can't I get that support from my peers here? They won't give me feedback or support, and they definitely don't want to see me succeed. They don't see my vision, and quite frankly, it does make me doubt myself. And that is going to mess with success. Achievement and self-doubt cannot coexist.

"So here I am, dealing with the same issues with the same type of people twenty years later. It's time for me to change. Otherwise, I'm going to have to really rethink my friends and possibly explore a more challenging and supportive professional life elsewhere. Unfortunately, if that is my path, I'll most likely run into these same situations again at some point, so why not 'grow it here' and learn from it?

"After all, wherever I land, I'll still have my suppositions and my bookshelves filled with journals of all of my notes, dreams, and theories. There are probably five to seven ideas worthy of world use. But what if the world doesn't think they're great? Well, there is my brain. If anyone saw how messy my desk was or could get into my brain, they would see all my ideas. I have to get them out. The question is, should I do that here, or somewhere else? Time will tell."

All she knew was that she had the opportunity to make these changes to see if it could improve her daily life and, perhaps, bolster her accomplishments. At the end of the day, she didn't have anything to lose! The next time she experienced the derision or dismissal of her co-workers, she determined that she would speak up for herself.

"Allis! It's lunchtime!"

Wow. What a day already. That was worth it. I feel empowered and have a much clearer idea about what I want to really feel and experience at work. After all, I'm there every day, all day, so I might as well enjoy it!

Allis stretched and yawned as if she was too busy to be bothered. One foot in front of the other, she was behind her mama and on her way to the kitchen. Allis purred as she brushed up against Silla.

"I love Saturdays," exclaimed Silla.

"How can it be 3 o'clock already?"

Silla finished her salad and decided she would go on a run before her shower. She had three hours until Jenna picked her up for the cooking lesson. With this morning's work, she would be able to enjoy a fun night cooking and connecting with friends. Tomorrow, she would visit her dad in the nursing home before her call with Michael J. Fox, the founder of the Michael J. Fox Foundation. She chairs a committee under the foundation to honor her father's life with Parkinson's disease. As members of the board, they headed back to the future to prepare for the upcoming board meeting. She had such incredible respect for Michael, who she grew up watching on TV. Now, she works with him several times a month, always in awe of his courage and his hope that they will find a cure.

In each meeting, he starts off with his motto, "To me, hope is informed optimism." With that, everyone is grounded in unity.

Yes, informed optimism, she thought. *The perfect theme for my weekend, and the upcoming week. I'm ready!*

SILLA'S REFLECTION & PLAN TO EMPOWER & ADVOCATE FOR HERSELF

Silla invites us to stop shrinking and allowing ourselves to be marginalized in these incredible careers we have earned. She learned that entering a traditionally male-dominated workforce after working towards and receiving her education, degrees, and scholarships is a big leap, and one she needed to powerfully embrace instead of shrinking away. It's not easy, and it takes more internal dialogue and planning to be intentional than anyone usually realizes. When she learned that she needed to make the change within herself to make the external forces change how they saw her, she was unstoppable. Follow along to get to know her thought process as she identified and readied herself for her next steps.

STEP 1 – AWARENESS

What was the situation?

After being dismissed, talked over, and left off the "credit" for the work she did, Silla was on fire! She was beside herself with anger towards the people she had worked with for years who kept doing this to her. As she expressed and worked through her anger, a lightbulb went off in her head: she realized that they would never change unless *she* changed her behavior, approach, and confidence. Once she realized that, she knew what had to happen next.

What could she do?

Silla did her best work as a scientist when she was mapping out her theories. She knew that if she could map out her feelings and the reactions she received versus the feelings and reactions she desired, then she could determine the steps she needed to take to change herself.

How was it affecting others?

Colleagues. If Silla stayed silent, she would actually be doing her colleagues a disservice by not contributing her knowledge and expertise. Additionally, she would have perpetuated the stigma and the behaviors, reactions, and impositions women face in male-dominated fields.

Women in S.T.E.A.M. There is a larger responsibility women have in S.T.E.A.M. industries: to represent themselves and others in a way that ensures that opportunities for future women are available. Additionally, the more women are active, involved, confident, and engaged in their field, the more men will become accustomed to the how and why of working with women. The collaboration and camaraderie that can be achieved positively impacts the company in many ways.

Silla. Clearly, Silla was letting her inner critic, her shy personality, and her self-doubt overtake her confidence and competence. In addition to the unpleasantness of being dismissed and talked over, she risked decreasing her competency and skills in her role because it impacted her self-esteem. Loss of confidence can cause a chain reaction that can lead to other negative outcomes.

STEP 2 – OPTIONS

How do others behave and what do they say or do to diminish Silla?

Ignored. It never mattered when Silla was in the lab. No one really went out of their way to say "Hello," or asked about her current assignment. Everyone had lunch together, and she headed to her cubby or ran errands.

Talked Over. When she shared ideas with a co-worker, Silla was often interrupted or talked over.

Dismissed. The results of her last breakthrough idea were supposed to be written up in a research article and submitted to a medical journal to represent the efforts of the whole team. It still had a chance, but the project's execution failed in the test phase. If it had been someone else, their mentor would have kept encouraging them and worked with them to get it over the finish line. Instead, when the testing failed, even though the discoveries were paramount to understanding many areas of viral distribution, her mentor dismissed her efforts and moved on with his own projects.

If Silla changed her actions and behaviors, what would Silla want to be the positive outcome?

Engaged and Included. Silla always felt like the last "woman" out and was ready for something different, something that would result in building engaging, life-long relationships with the people she cherished.

Respected. Feeling disrespected was the worst feeling. She had worked at her lab long enough to be a respected figure, but that hadn't happened yet. Perhaps being more involved and sharing her thoughts and ideas with more confidence would earn her some respect.

Heard. Silla was tired of being talked over and dismissed in meetings when she had something to share. She definitely needed some internal dialogue changes to give her the confidence to speak with the other members of her team and during meetings.

Supported and Encouraged. The longer she spent in this male-dominated field, the more difficult it became to find the support network she needed. She was going to find a new mentor and new sponsor.

STEP 3 – RISK v. REWARD

There are risks and rewards to every action we take or don't take.

Overcoming her shyness and increasing her confidence were two areas Silla discovered she needed to strengthen.

SHYNESS

How did Silla's shyness show up in her everyday work life?

Whenever she walked into the boardroom or an office room filled with multiple colleagues, the butterflies in her stomach were relentless. She would nod her head in greeting, rush to her seat, and avoid attracting notice. There, she kept her head in her notebook, writing notes until the meeting started and pretending to be busy.

What made Silla feel that there was a lack of significance in her work?

Historically, it was difficult for Silla to speak or even offer to speak. If she had a thought and moved to say something, people tended to dismiss her, especially men. She wondered if it was because she's a woman. She's shorter. She's quieter. In a room of all men, how would she command attention? So, when she did get the courage to speak, she waited until the end of the meeting to say anything. And, then, she was dismissed because everyone wanted to leave the meeting.

What benefits arise from Silla overcoming her shyness?

Silla's listening skills set her apart from her colleagues. Unlike others, who react on impulse instead of responding professionally, Silla was known for her ability to calmly respond and take thoughtful action. She only said things when they mattered and when she could contribute. People really knew she cared. She has an awareness of everything around her at all times and can see around corners when it comes to avoiding costly mistakes. In the right crowd, when she did pull up her "big girl pants" and speak, people listened and took her seriously.

CONFIDENCE

Where does Silla's confidence level rank right now, and where would she want it?

People would describe Silla as a woman with an air of confidence who is comfortable with herself and does not doubt the value or quality of her work. Silla would describe herself as steadfast in her work and career, but shaky when it comes to building relationships, speaking, voicing her thoughts, and standing up for herself. Although she has no issue standing up for others, as she has had to do so in the lab on behalf of younger scientists, when it comes to standing up for herself, she would rather crawl under a lab table and avoid it.

Silla is not taken seriously because people cannot read her mind, she doesn't "vouch" for herself, and her male mentors consistently critique her lack of courage and confidence, which make it difficult for her to be recognized for her efforts, even though her work product, her theories, and her creative approach to problem solving are notable.

Silla needs "Clarity" to determine her confident future.

Silla has always been introverted and has neither boasted about herself nor tried to put on airs about her abilities in the company of others; she spent that time being introspective. For Silla, clarity is the key to achieving her goal to be a "Sensational Scientist," because it's the first attribute she embodies when working on any project. When you start out with clear intentions, clear directions, clear observations, and a clear slate, you are free to create, theorize, and test anything and everything.

STEP 4 – APPROACH

What was the best approach?

The first key step for Silla to examine how she behaves today and how she would prefer to operate tomorrow is to start with a blank slate, evaluating everything about herself: her likes, her dislikes, opportunities for improvement or enhancement, and anything else she can think of.

1. **List** current positive and negative attributes.
2. **Document** how the "new" Silla operates, engages, communicates, and stands up for herself.
3. **Identify** the verbal and nonverbal ways she can convey the type of presence that she wants to embody and start practicing in the mirror, in the car, in the shower.
4. **Practice** makes perfect. Some skills and traits need to grow with you.

STEP 5 – AGENT FOR CHANGE

What can I and will I do to change my approach, behavior, and confidence level?

Engage. Clearly, Silla is the quietest one in the lab at all times. Reaching out to say "hello" would go a long way to building some camaraderie.

Speak Up. When thoughts come into Silla's mind or when she has something to say, she needs to pull up her "big girl pants," push her shoulders back, hold her head high, and speak up. She already knows there is a select group that sincerely pays attention to her when she does speak.

Sit in the Front of the Room. While she loves being in the back of the meeting room so she can doodle, make checklists, and stay under the radar, she really can't equate the value of writing notes to the value of connecting with those around her. Instead of cowering, rushing to the back of the room, and shrinking into the chair to be avoided at all costs, she should claim one of the front seats, engage, and speak when she has something to say.

Female Mentor & Female Sponsor. Silla realized with the journal entry that she hasn't found a good mentor yet, she needs more support and direction. She will seek out a female mentor in the S.T.E.A.M. field, hopefully in science, to mentor her, even if that woman is from outside the organization. Quality matters more than location. Additionally, she will look for a sponsor in her current organization, who will be her professional advocate and support her when engaging with those who do not yet know her or find her to be stand-offish because of her introverted personality.

Get Social. She loves her Friday night ritual, but she could dedicate an hour before her sunset soak to spending time with her co-workers and getting to know people better.

Stand Up for Self. On Friday, during the presentation, her co-worker steamrolled over her, took the credit for the outcome, and continued on as though she didn't exist. She couldn't help but wonder if it's because she is Asian. With the outrage around the fact that COVID originated in China, hate crimes against Asians have dramatically increased. Her co-workers could have unconscious bias against her and not even know it themselves. Is it because she is short and female? Or could it even be that, because she is intelligent, they are all threatened by her talents?

GAYLE'S REFLECTIONS ON CLARITY TO INCREASE CONFIDENCE

In a male-dominated workforce, it is so easy for women to be overlooked, like Silla experienced. Once we have clarity in our minds about who we are and the role we play in our profession, we are able to stand up for ourselves. Our voices need to be heard, for the sake of the women of today and tomorrow. In recent years, gender equality in pay and opportunities have become an issue for political and equal rights platforms.

The Path to Parity for 2030 seems to be the benchmark for US organizations to achieve gender parity in the workplace by setting goals for 40% - 50% of women to sit at the table in positions equal to those of their male peers and with equal pay. That's a lofty goal, given women are still outnumbered by men in the workplace, and not just by a little. So, how can society usher in a path to parity and greatly change the culture across all boardrooms and offices? What holds women in S.T.E.A.M. (WiSTEAM) back? According to Tech Jury, reasons include *"...gender bias and derogatory behavior in the workplace, unequal growth opportunities with male co-workers to [earning a] lesser wage for the same position."*

Compared to women, men are more comfortable and confident when it comes to taking calculated risks in their careers. It's been reported that men apply for promotions when they have 30% of the required skill level or competence, while women wait until they have achieved 80% - 90% of the requirements of the job description. Now that the "cat is out of the bag," let's change that statistic. The next time you want a promotion or see a job description calling your name, apply for it, no matter your level of experience or skill. The worst that could happen is they don't call you. Rejection no longer needs to stop us in our tracks. We waste too much time trying to "fill our resumes enough" to be qualified. I say, if you are 30% qualified, you are 100% qualified. For most of our jobs, we learn everything on the job anyway.

Now, clearly, there are exceptions to this rule, such as a job opening for a crane operator, machine operator, surgeon, and such; if you intend to take on those jobs, you should definitely be 100% skilled. For the most part, those looking for promotions in their office jobs, management positions, and the like don't necessarily have to meet 100% of the qualifications that women typically hold themselves to when seeking to achieve their next goal.

When it comes to communication and standing up for ourselves, we need to use our voice to be heard. Stop being quiet. Yes, men need to respect a woman's point of view and let us speak for ourselves. And for those who are silencing us, undermining us, or not listening, stop! Silencing us, not listening or not considering our solutions, opinions, thoughts, or refusing to support our roles is not practicing inclusion. Even worse is when men take credit for a female co worker's suggestion, proposal, or solution. This happens all too frequently.

Studies show that when there are diverse groups of people working together on boards, in organizations, and on teams, there is a tremendous advantage and increase in profits because of the varied experiences, perspectives, and levels of expertise brought to the table.

However, we don't achieve goals or earn gender equality when we just sit back and take it or sit around and blame men. As a trusted advisor, I frequently coach men on how to act in a more inclusive fashion when it comes to diversifying their teams. My work is a two-goal approach, because it's important to advise the individual on their goal along with the goals of the organization—inclusivity can only be effectively implemented system-wide, and therefore needs to become part of the fabric of the culture.

Silla values "Clarity" as a contributing factor to her success. During my online class, "Clarity" is one of the five pillars I teach because, in my own career, I discovered that when I have clarity, I'm empowered to look at my current situation, identify the roadblocks holding me back, and learn how to successfully move forward. Now, I may "fail forward," but I know that I will find my way up.

Once Silla thought more clearly about what was important to her, the actions that she was taking that contributed to the negative outcomes she didn't want, and what she wanted to change, she was empowered to use her voice and design a new blueprint for her career, along with a roadmap for developing her new behaviors. Once we are empowered, we can discern what we truly want in our lives and visualize our goals and how to achieve them. To keep it simple, I've designed

"Gayle's Prescription to Finding Clarity": 1. Process 2. Plan 3. Refine 4. Repeat

GAYLE'S PRESCRIPTION TO FINDING CLARITY

1. Consider what is holding you back from achieving your dreams and exceeding your expectations of yourself. Like Silla, this requires some hard work, because you need to take a hard look at yourself and identify things/people/places/etc. And you can't blame others. This is where you must be accountable for your own good, and only you can truly change negative outcomes to positive outcomes.

2. Understand your start and end points when it comes to your career. Brainstorm your professional and personal aspirations. Identify your skills, tools, and strengths. Jot down the skills you possess that make your heart sing. Match up possible career paths that will incorporate one or both. Then, follow the Clarity Formula above with different roles until you find your ideal path.

3. Identify your roadblocks that prevent you from starting or succeeding. Fill in any gaps you may have in expertise or time.

4. Compose a 90-day plan and one-year plan that get you from where you are today to where you want to go and grow in the future.

5. Hold yourself accountable and find a trusted accountability partner who will encourage, support, and guide you to achieve your goals and design your future.

CAREER RESOURCES FROM GAYLE

Perseverance, curiosity, grit, determination, and a strong work ethic will get you far. Struggling with indecision in your career? Consider my online course in two formats: self-guided or group mastermind. You'll be empowered to take calculated risks in your career to reinvent your professional life, whether you're seeking employee retention and growth within an organization or exploring new opportunities. Visit https://www.gaylekeller.org/digitalcourse for more information.

PILLAR 2: DECISIVENESS

TYRIQA, THE DECISIVE TECHNOLOGIST

"Listen, Tyriqa. It doesn't matter if you created an app in high school. When it comes to tech, you will have to climb the career ladder the same way the rest of us have. It's taken me ten years to get where I am. There are only so many seats at the table, and you won't be in one any time soon," Ethel warned her.

"I just thought that, since we are going over my performance review, now would be a good time to discuss any possible promotions, or to get career guidance from you," Tyriqa stated matter-of-factly and as politely as she could, unobtrusively adjusting her hearing aid to ensure she caught every word out of Ethel's mouth. She quickly realized that she was not being supported by her boss. She would have to tread carefully here.

"No. You're not ready yet."

Tyriqa stayed quiet, stunned at the turn of the conversation. She had never been so poorly treated. Being a Black American and a woman, she was used to treading water in some business and social settings, but these waters were rougher than she had expected. She had just been awarded the company's Innovator of the Year award for her project, and she was feeling really good about her year, accomplishments, and contributions to the team and organization. She was so motivated to plan for her future here, knowing there was so much more she could give. In a male-dominated tech field, her boss was one of the few women in her department—and she had just trashed her motivation. Tyriqa was going to be squished under her thumb unless something changed.

"You can go now, Tyriqa. I have another meeting."

Tyriqa walked out, shoulders squared. She said nothing.

It felt like I was outside of my body, watching this happen. There was really nothing I could've said that wouldn't confirm that I was her subordinate. Which I am, but I wasn't going to give her the satisfaction, Tyriqa thought to herself.

"Can you believe that, Momma?" Tyriqa asked as she tenderized the beef for the stew that night.

"Mmm. I can, and I cannot, all at the same time. You have been working so hard, we hardly have you home for dinner. You know, Tyriqa, this usually happens when people feel threatened by someone."

"Threatened? I'm just doing my job as best as I can. Why would she feel threatened? I've respected and admired her all this time. I really thought she would be one of those types of bosses that empower their female team members, not tear them down."

"Unfortunately, it usually comes from the people you don't expect."

Tyriqa's mom dealt with plenty of unsupportive bosses when she worked for NASA in the days when John Glenn had been launched to orbit the earth. She personally witnessed the work of the three Black women who were the mathematicians behind his successful flight. It took until 2016 for them to be properly recognized for their acclaimed work when the movie *Hidden Figures* was released.

"Momma, years later, we are still fighting for seats at the table, even with my own Black, female boss. This entire experience does not sit well with me. In fact, I'm furious. My girlfriends have better bosses than this. Several of them *are* their own boss. All I hear from them is how great it is to be out of tech because women in other fields are finally empowering each other instead of competing. That's what I want. Collaboration, guidance, mentorship. Instead, Ethel flatlined me in four sentences."

During their conversation, Tyriqa recalled a book she had recently read: *Activate Your Money* by Janine Firpo. It educates women on how to align their money and investments with their values. Janine Firpo inspired her from the first time she'd read her book, and especially strongly now. She, too, was a woman in tech who followed her calling, branching out from her tech background to become a values-aligned investor, angel investor, and social innovator. Janine found her voice and calling in the male-dominated tech industry, becoming one of the first mobile money experts.

Tyriqa shared the book's key points with her mother. "If I could only channel Janine's disposition and relate it to my end goal: confront my boss, and follow my aspirations to make them a reality."

"*Cheers*, Tyriqa! I'm so proud of you!"

Dylan and Tyriqa clinked glasses at the quarterly company dinner party. Finally, they had time to sit and talk, just the two of them. Dylan was in her business unit, but he worked for a different director. While they did not work on projects together, they would commiserate when needed, and they celebrated as much as possible. Life was too short not to have a good friend at work.

When they met four years ago, they hit it off immediately. Dylan had been caught in the rain, and she had asked him if his curly blond hair always behaved that way—disheveled. His puppy-dog brown eyes were sincere, and he had the biggest heart. Their conversations were easy and flowed smoothly, like the pour of a beautiful and delicious red cabernet. They talked about everything under the sun, and they had their little spats every now and again. She supposed one could call him her "work husband."

"So, tell me, what's it like to be 'Innovator of the Year,' Tyriqa?"

"Winning that award was such a surprise! I'm really excited. Between you and me, I love the way it looks on my desk—and my online profile," she laughed.

"How about that standing ovation?" Dylan asked as he raised his glass, clinking it against hers.

"I still have chills. It was awesome."

"So many people admire, respect, and like you, Tyriqa. You should be really proud of yourself."

"Hey, Ethel!" Dylan shouted across the table as her boss walked past them.

Ethel sauntered over, unsure of what was to happen. Tyriqa hadn't had a chance to update Dylan about her review meeting.

"What do you think of our 'Innovator of the Year' here?" Dylan probed.

Oh no, she thought.

"Well, you know, there's a lot of work ahead of her. My advice, Tyriqa, is that you follow the KISS method. Do you know what that is?" Ethel's tone was condescending. "Keep it simple, stupid."

She sauntered away as if she were a seagull, flying in, dumping on their heads, and flying off. Their jaws felt as if they were on the floor.

"What the…?" Dylan asked, flabbergasted.

"Well, at least now I have a witness to remind me that it's not just me," Tyriqa replied.

"What's going on?" He asked with sincere empathy.

"I have no idea. I just know that she used my review meeting to put me in my place. She discouraged me from getting my hopes up about advancing my career, saying it took her ten years to get in her position, and it would take me longer because she wasn't going anywhere."

"Crap."

Tyriqa proceeded to share the details with Dylan. He was dumbfounded and enraged. She hadn't even processed her feelings yet, and he was ready to "take her out back."

"Are you thinking of transferring to a different director?"

"I haven't even thought about that. I was so shocked; I just can't get my head around it. I thought my winning the award would have indicated a great review was coming, but she made me feel small and insignificant. She even said, 'Just because you built an app in high school doesn't mean you get a fast pass to the top rung.'"

"Tyriqa, that is beyond awful. I'm so sorry. You do know that people who behave that way are threatened by what you offer the company. She is shaking in her boots. Trust me. That award put a target on your back. You need to keep your head on a swivel where she's concerned."

"Dylan, when we started to work together, I was so excited she was my boss. I had visions that she would be a female mentor who was supportive and empowering, who understood where her employees came from and how hard life could be. She's the exact opposite, and part of the female sabotage movement that's been happening forever. She might as well be a man."

"I hate to say it, but it sounds like workplace bullying. What are you going to do?"

"Workplace bullying? Is that a thing? Bullying isn't just restricted to school playgrounds?"

"No. It's alive and well in workplaces, too, depending on the culture and the leadership."

"That's just great. I don't know what I'm going to do. It all just started happening yesterday, and I'm still processing everything. What are my options?"

Dylan jumped in his chair to scoot it closer to her. "Well, you could apply for a transfer to be on my team or another business unit."

"Don't you think I would be blocklisted?" Tyriqa asked.

"Maybe, but usually directors can sniff this stuff out. Trust me, we are not the only ones she's expressed her disdain to. I'll keep my ears open."

"You know, I have so many girlfriends who are supported and empowered in their careers. They either work for their 'dream boss' or they are their own 'dream boss.' Maybe working in tech isn't a good fit for me anymore. I'm a go-getter. Being tenacious is how I've been successful my whole life in this industry. It's how I designed and built my app for handbags when I was in high school."

"I'd hate for you to leave, Tyriqa," Dylan said, his big, puppy-dog eyes pleading with her. "It's good to have options and keep them open. I'll scout around my department and see what I can uncover. Either way, it sounds like you are ready to reinvent yourself."

"Reinvention! Yes, I love that word! I know I'm not going to stay under Ethel's watch for ten years and struggle on each rung. Maybe this was the kick I needed to take a step forward. I'll do a deep-dive assessment tomorrow at home and see what comes out of it. Thank God it's Friday!"

The next day, at home, as Tyriqa worked through the assessment, she said out loud to herself, "I wasn't expecting to go into my truest, deepest desires involving finding a new job so soon, but honestly, it would be refreshing to be in a sales environment buzzing with energy, adrenaline oozing from aggressive goals, and full of rewarding successes! Now, that would be a real treat!"

As Tyriqa spoke to herself, her dog's head popped up from the red fluffy bed at the mention of a treat. He whimpered.

"Oh, Denzel, you would hear me say that. C'mon, let's get you a treat. Peanut butter or pumpkin? Have a preference?"

He barked at "pumpkin." The German Shepherd kept her company in her room whenever she came home for the day. The hardest part of leaving for college had been saying good-bye to Denzel. The tears had fallen harder for him than her parents. He loved her boomeranging home again, and she loved his company.

"Hey, Tyriqa! How is your 'reinvention assessment' coming?"

"Mom and Dad, I didn't expect it to go in the direction it's going. It's been quite interesting—and a little upsetting."

"What have you determined?"

"I haven't, yet." As she gave Denzel the treat, she poured herself a cup of tea and headed to her favorite spot in the living room.

"When I dove deep into my heart about what I really wanted, I found myself somewhere else doing tech, or software sales, because I love tech, and I love being more involved with people." She sat down with a big "humph."

"Really? That's a shift!" Dad said.

"I guess I wasn't thinking of a new job so soon, and I thought the award would anchor me here for much longer."

"But, T, you've mentioned that before, so it's not out of the blue," Mom said.

"True."

Dad started and stopped. "T, have you thought about addressing your disappointment with your boss?"

"Hmmm. Not really. I'm trying to keep that out of my mind."

"People do have bad days, and maybe she never had anyone supportive in her life," Dad continued. "Sometimes, strong people are called to 'lead up.'"

"Lead up? What is that?"

"In this type of situation, people can take things the wrong way. Or perhaps it's intentional, and, if so, then she wasn't taught a better way. You could take this opportunity to open the door for the two of you to form a more empowering relationship."

"Is that even possible? Dylan mentioned workplace bullying."

"Anything is possible. Personally, I would just hate for you to leave without ever sharing your concerns. Otherwise, how will she learn?" Mom interjected.

"Hmmm. So, you're suggesting I have a meeting with her to share my thoughts about how I want to advance in this company, which does not mean taking over her job, but, rather, learning from her. Additionally, tell her that I didn't appreciate her review being so condescending and disrespectful. And as for KISS, she should never say that again. It doesn't reflect well on her."

"Yes. When you approach an issue like this professionally, with a mild and collaborative tone, you can get a lot accomplished. It can go one of two ways. First," Dad explained animatedly, "She could reply professionally, apologize, and see your side. A perfect ending would be that she offers to mentor you. Second, it could go sideways, and she could get annoyed or angry."

"I don't want that again. I can see what you're saying. I don't know where anything stands right now. Let me think it over."

"Absolutely. Either way, your mom and I support your decision."

"Just one thing, T," Mom said. "If you don't take this step to talk with her, you are not giving her a chance to correct her behavior towards her future employees. And, considering the bigger picture, you would not be lending your hand to the women of tomorrow in your field."

"That's deep, Mom. Thanks."

"I know. When we have these opportunities, we have to take the high road for the betterment of the future for everyone. She may not be the perfect boss right now, but maybe she can learn from you. Either way, you'll know where you stand and what's possible with her."

"Ugh." Tyriqa trudged up the steep hill at a trot, huffing and puffing. After the talk with her mom and dad, she needed some fresh air. She pretty much hated running, but when she was super stressed, she sprinted up the hills during her fast-paced walk to burn off some of the stress. It wasn't fun, but it was always exhilarating on the way down. She called Dylan to meet up with her for a run and for some much-needed moral support.

"What am I going to do?" she asked herself out loud as she descended the hill, as the birds chirped and the cold air rose off of the lake. "If I stay, what has to happen? What do I need? What do I need to do? If I'm going to leave, what are the steps I should take? What should I have so I can be ready to leave? What do I need to do to leave?"

"Why does taking the high road have to be so hard, Dylan?" Tyriqa asked, pausing for a moment to adjust her hearing aid, as it had become dislodged during her run.

"Because it's called the 'high road,' T. " Dylan shook his head with major empathy for Tyriqa. It was comforting to Tyriqa to have his support and concern. "Not everyone has what it takes to go for it. You're taking one for the team."

"I'm taking one for all womanhood, Dylan! That's the only reason I'm doing it. It would be so much easier to get a job, leave, and never talk to her again, but I'm called to be better."

R-E-S-P-E-C-T.

Find out what it means to me!

R-E-S-P-E-C-T.

It was Friday, after lunch, and Tyriqa was in her office's private restroom. Aretha Franklin belted out her letters and oohs and aahs in her "RESPECT" song through T's earphones. Tyriqa jumped up and down, pumped her arms up, looked up at the ceiling, and got into her power stance, which she had developed after watching all the episodes of Wonder Woman.

She was getting ready to meet with Ethel. She fluffed her hair, added blush, and freshened her lipstick. Red. Red lipstick had magic powers, especially when coupled with Tina Turner.

"Pump me up!" she shouted, but not so loudly that people in the hall would hear her.

She fluffed her hair and took one more spin in front of the mirror to make sure she was looking good and powerful. She wore her favorite suit with a red v-neck blouse and a black blazer. She felt the power. After all, studies report that whoever wears the darkest color in the room is "the one who is in charge."

"Oh, yeah, I'm in charge today. I'm going to make life easier for every woman that comes here after me."

"Hey, Denzel!" Tyriqa bent down to pet the 95-pound pup.

"Phew. I'm glad to be home," she said as she slipped off her jacket and boots, heading to the kitchen to make a cup of tea.

"I thought someone was home," Mom exclaimed. "You're home early. Nice to see you."

Tyriqa's mother kissed her on the forehead.

"Yes, I figured if I was going up against Ol' Ethel, I could leave early to decompress."

"Ohhhh. You talked to her? Wow. What a huge step."

"Yes, Mom, it was a huge step for me, and for all womankind."

"All womankind? What is this I hear? Have you saved the planet from men?" Dad asked, trying to control his belly laugh. He was always a good sport and empowered the women in his life, especially Tyriqa and her mom, every chance he could.

"She talked to her boss today," Mom interjected a little too enthusiastically. It was clear to Tyriqa they had been wondering about her decision.

"Ohhh. And?" Dad replied, tossing a glance at T while she filled her mug with chamomile tea; already, the warmth of the steam was soothing her.

"Well. I wasn't fired. In short, I shared that I was displeased with the tone and the message I understood during my review because of my belief in empowering people. I stressed that I wasn't the type to 'take over' someone's job and had been really excited about joining her team because of the mentorship program the company offers. Plus, I really, really wanted to learn all I could from her because I respected her so much. I expressed that I felt disdain coming from her all of last week, and that the KISS comment was out of left field, unfair, and unprofessional. I was just honest."

"Annnndddd," Mom and Dad said in unison. "Sounds good so far."

"She didn't see why I was complaining. This is 'the way tech runs.' She has too much other work to do to mentor me. Except, she did want to share that I should stop trying to one-up everyone. I almost lost it, but kept it together and said, 'I have high regard for work ethic and excellent work product. I only believe in performing my best, so if others are bothered or threatened by it, that's their issue, not mine.' Then, her phone rang. She answered it, and I left. So, as of this moment, I'm actively looking for my next job in tech sales, and I can't wait!"

"Oh, Tyriqa! I'm so sorry. I'm proud of you," Mom said, patting my hand.

"Me, too," Dad agreed, putting his hand on my arm and giving me one of his famous supportive sidehugs.

"I remember you both always saying a leopard cannot change their spots. I gave her a chance, she roared, and I'm outta there. She's not my responsibility."

"Even though you didn't make progress with her, you definitely took a giant step for all women today," Dad said, beaming with pride.

TYRIQA'S REFLECTION & PLAN TO REINVENT HERSELF

STEP 1 – AWARENESS

What was the situation?

Tyriqa started her career in her teens and worked hard to continue to achieve successes at every turn in her journey. When she started working for her current company, she was already well-known for an app she built in her teen years. She felt lucky to work for a woman of color, like herself, and had great hopes that she would be mentored by her and be able to follow in her footsteps one day. Unfortunately, her boss didn't have any inclination to nurture her employees or help them. Rather, she thought of them as laborers that served the company. Once Tyriqa realized this during her review, she knew she would be a small fish swimming upstream unless something changed.

How was it affecting others?

Work. If her boss was treating her this way, there's a good chance that she also treated other people similarly. That means that others working for Ethel were probably not achieving their full potential either. Collectively, and not to be dramatic, that means there could be an entire department that is not performing to their best abilities because their talents, efforts, and expertise are being squashed by someone who feels they must be in control. At the end of the day, the bottom line, company profits, and employees are impacted the most.

Family. The longer Tyriqa needed to work to pay off her loans with her current salary, the longer she would be living with her mom and dad. That was not a long-term goal she planned at any given point in her life.

Tyriqa. Whenever people work with bullies, the experience can do a number on their confidence and self-esteem, as well as amplify the voice of their inner critic. Tyriqa needed to handle this less than ideal situation one way or another or she would be miserable in her career.

STEP 2 – OPTIONS

Like many women in S.T.E.A.M., Tyriqa worked extremely hard to earn her position in her company. As she considered how to handle the situation with her boss, she first needed to identify what she wanted to change in her work environment and career.

SEEK EMPOWERMENT & SUPPORT. Growing up, Tyriqa was surrounded by people who supported her. Her parents impressed upon her that a college education was important, and that she could have any job she wanted. They did not pigeonhole Tyriqa with toy choices and work choices that were intended for boys or girls, which gave Tyriqa opportunities that she sees some of her friends didn't have. She was an avid video game player, which inspired her to learn coding to create a simple video game. This ultimately led her to program an app that served as an online marketplace to sell handbags. Apple loved her app so much, they asked her to charge $1.99 for each download.

She steadily saved money for college. Her parents put great emphasis on the importance of philanthropy and giving back to her community. For every paycheck earned, she deposited most into her college savings, contributed to charity, and put some aside for specific needs and wants. She avoided those who were negative or unsupportive.

With the support that she received throughout her life, she knew she had an advantage. She also understood that the gifts given to her—the empowerment and support she received from her family—were gifts she needed to share with others to give them a hand up, too. She wanted to create more opportunities for women in her field and to empower and support them, efforts she would benefit from herself as well.

MAKE A DIFFERENCE. Throughout her life, Tyriqa felt called to a special purpose and put her trust in following that calling. She knew she needed to forget the naysayers and surround herself with empowering students, teachers, family members, and colleagues. In essence, she created her ideal culture within her own community, which is why her handbag app was a success. Now, she clearly was no longer working in her ideal culture, and that was an important insight relative to her career and next steps.

In her career, there were plenty of ways to make a difference. After all, technology advances society and improves lives. Plus, the time she spent volunteering with organizations—specifically Girls Who Code and Black Girls Code—definitely made an impact on the lives of girls and women with dreams like Tyriqa.

Receiving the "Innovator of the Year Award" at her job out of everyone in her entire organization affirmed that she had made a difference in this job.

FACE CONFLICTS. Tyriqa wasn't one to run away from difficult problems, and she was no stranger to addressing difficult situations. But can anyone really nurture a relationship with a workplace bully? Is it possible, or even worth the effort, to try?

"Okay, girl, you've got to figure this out. What is in your heart? Make sure you pay attention to your instincts and gut during this exercise. Listen to the whispers." Tyriqa encouraged herself.

She also realized that positive self-talk and self-motivation were key to her success.

STEP 3 – RISK v. REWARD

There are risks and rewards to every action we take or don't take.

Should Tyriqa stay in her current role, or leave the company?

Tyriqa's reputation preceded her resume and first interview. The Handbag App was a smashing success, and once everyone found out about Apple's fee arrangement, her name and reputation as a "tech phenom" spread like wildfire through the metropolitan area. It was almost like a football draft for college players, except it was a one-woman draft for a tech genius. The company execs wanted to hire her without meeting her; HR disapproved and started the proper hiring and inquiry process. Tyriqa didn't let them down. Within two years, she became the recipient of the Innovator of the Year Award. Companies and recruiters started to call to ask if she was ready to change jobs yet.

Tyriqa has always been a very loyal employee. It will be difficult for her to leave, especially after getting an award. It wouldn't exactly look very professional, leaving after receiving such an honor, but others do it all the time. Moreover, her boss, Ethel, would never put two and two together and recognize that her callous attitude towards her employee opened Tyriqa's mind to leaving. Before Ethel's smackdown, she had no intention of even thinking about going elsewhere.

Is the grass greener on the other side?

Tyriqa occasionally daydreams about taking on a sales job in tech because she favors working with people more than code. The role would perfectly blend her two greatest strengths: tech and people. She knows her tech, obviously, and people consistently recognize her interpersonal skills when working with team members, vendors, and executives. It might be the right time for a career change. In sales, there aren't any glass ceilings, and income is based on trust, relationships, tenacity, and hard work.

Could working for a different department be enough?

It's disappointing to see the differences among how directors treat their team members. Dylan's director was fair, respectful, and grateful for his work. He had quarterly mentoring meetings with him to make sure he was on track to achieve his goals. How did Ethel miss the mark on this? Tyriqa had really counted on receiving good mentorship when taking this job, as there hadn't been any similar opportunities at the law firm she worked for while in college, where she basically stamped consecutive numbers on documents until her wrists froze and eyes bled. That job was bound to make her dumber and be a dead-end. Nevertheless, she appreciated the money during an economic downturn. No job was beneath her, something her parents instilled in her from a young age.

What was the greatest risk for Tyriqa if she stayed?

Staying at a job without mentorship was detrimental to the future of Tyriqa's career. She needed someone to confide in and to talk to about challenges, goals, achievements, and the steps required to make it to the next promotion. Mentorship programs in larger companies are known to have significantly positive impacts on their employees, regardless of gender. Reports show that employees who are mentored from the first day achieve more and advance more in the following five years than employees working for companies where mentorship programs do not exist.

Tyriqa would not wait around to climb the next nine rungs one at a time. It didn't make any sense, especially since she just broke the first two rungs and dropped to zero by being a member of Ethel's team.

STEP 4 – APPROACH

If Tyriqa is going to stay, she needs to figure out how to address, navigate, and—hopefully—make the workplace bullying situation better.

1. **UPDATE DYLAN.** In this situation, it's important for Tyriqa to keep Dylan in the know about her situation. He is usually her voice of reason and will tell the absolute truth. His counsel is the whole advantage of having a "work husband," isn't it?

2. **ADDRESS CONFLICT.** Tyriqa's mom was right. It was her responsibility to offer a hand to someone else who may never have had one—fortunately, and unfortunately. Fortunately, because so many people helped and guided her along the way, and she loved opportunities to pay it forward. Unfortunately, because she had to get the strength and power to address this giant, ugly elephant in the room. She needed the next step to be positive and to empower her to stand in her sovereignty and agency, which avoided giving her power away. It wasn't easy, but she made herself do it for her own future, and for the future of all women!

3. **READ AND FEEL THE ROOM.** Everyone needs to call on their instinctive "feelers" to make the best decision on how to approach a problem or situation. Tyriqa remembered this for her meeting with Ethel. All Tyriqa's senses needed to be on alert to read Ethel's nonverbal cues, her sincerity, commitment, and other related "tells." Tyriqa hoped her nerves wouldn't get the best of her.

STEP 5 – AGENT FOR CHANGE

Support & Collaboration. Why in the world didn't Ethel see the importance of mentoring Tyriqa? Every Black woman who made something of herself mentored others; she helped other people along and other people helped her along in her industry. By not mentoring anyone, Ethel dismissed the future careers of women all over the world and ensured that they would keep getting stuck. Tyriqa daydreamed about what she would say if she moved out of the department. *I'll be sure to KISS when I explain 'paying it forward' to you in my exit interview, Ethel.*

Promotions & Accolades. Clearly, Tyriqa is a high achiever and is motivated by receiving recognition for superior work. She would do well in a workplace that had opportunities for advancement, awards, and opportunities to pay it forward.

Tech & Sales Role. She definitely would look for a sales position in tech. It may be a step down, until she proves her worth to her new employer, but Tyriqa was willing to weather such a setback. She's young enough that starting something new would still be worth the short-term sacrifice, as long as she is in the right place.

Empowering Culture. Tyriqa desired to be in an environment where she was part of a well-oiled relationship machine. She aspired to have mentors to the right of her and mentees to the left of her, to be a part of a workplace culture that was collaborative, supportive, inclusive, productive, and successful. She needed to study the culture and get some "intel" on each company to make sure it's legit and that it would be a good fit for her. Culture was key!

Female Mentor & Female Sponsor. There must be a mentor-mentee and sponsorship program in place that everyone supported. Tyriqa had big plans and needed support for her anticipated career growth. She won't always get answers from her mom and dad. Now would be a good time for her to crack open *Strategize to Win* by Carla Harris, a book recommended to her because of Carla's brilliant explanation as to why every working person needs "currency sponsors"—both a "performance currency" sponsor and a "relationship currency" sponsor—to speak positively on that person's behalf behind closed doors as they "measure the person's subjectivity" (as Carla says) so they can become better known within the company and, ultimately, get ahead in their career.

Pay Increase. Tyriqa's current job paid her well; however, there was a cap to her potential for growth. When she was hired, she meticulously reviewed her income and expenses, outlining a budget for living with her parents and another for living on her own. If she started living on her own, it would take her three more years to buy a condo, so she opted to stay with her parents to save money, pay off college loans, and pay down her car loan. Her parents were always easy to get along with. On the nights she came home at a regular time from work, they cooked dinner and enjoyed a glass of wine from their favorite vineyard together.

No Ceiling. In sales, commission was at least 40% of the compensation plan, and if the quotas were exceeded, there were bonuses. Tyriqa wouldn't be restricted to making a stagnant salary year after year. She would move into sales to crush the ten-step ladder—and the glass ceiling in tech today. She wanted to make the maximum amount of money, earn the most promotions, and receive the most awards for "Salesperson of the Year."

GAYLE'S REFLECTIONS ON DECISIVENESS

The gender gap in technology is still quite prevalent. And the gap within start-up funding is an eyesore, especially if you are a woman of color, like one of my Theodora Speaks™ podcast guests, Jacquelle Amankonah Horton. Jacquelle is in the top one percent of the two percent of black female executives breaking the mold, which is something she's equal parts proud of and frustrated about. As a new mother, Jacquelle left Silicon Valley during the global pandemic to embrace "The Great Reinvention" and launched "Fave," a social platform and marketplace that allows engagement between fans and music artists alike.

For 20+ years, I've been a woman in technology, and I *love* technology, but I did face gender inequality firsthand. If we want to see gender inclusion in our lifetime, women need to include other qualified women on their journey as they climb the ranks. Given there are only so many seats at the table, women need to stop bullying and cannibalizing each other as they excel in the workplace. Far too often, women feel threatened by other women and, therefore, they do not help nurture top talent as they build their teams.

I invest my time coaching women to focus on building out their personal portfolios while also harnessing the values they seek from other women and invite them to be on their professional team. One of the women I work with switched roles within her organization and is going through a reinvention in her career in a mid-level position into a managerial role. I helped her harness her experience to create a portfolio highlighting her best work that proves she is the right candidate for the position. Another suggestion is for women to mentor and sponsor other qualified women, help them climb the ranks, and shake the generational tone of "you need to figure it out alone, and then we'll see if you have what it takes to succeed." The quit rate for WiSTEM is approximately 53.6%!

GAYLE'S PRESCRIPTION TO BECOME DECISIVE

Together, let's turn this statistic around and foster a welcoming, inclusive environment for our fellow women in the ranks. Here are some ideas on how we can contribute to the movement.

1. Above all else, no matter the situation, respect yourself and your values, and be respected. Inclusion does not exist in a toxic work environment. If you voice your concerns, offer ways to improve yourself, and recommend a solution(s) for the problem, and you find that nothing changes, then it's time to re-evaluate your decision to work in a toxic environment. Verbally abusive bullying is unacceptable and disrespectful. Bullying

and toxicity in the workplace can lead to emotional and physical unwellness, which leads to lack of productivity and profitability, which does not bode well for the employee—or the employer.

2. Break down your indecision by creating a pros / cons list. Review your list, hone in on what makes you happy, and start to blueprint your strategy on how to achieve your goals.

3. Set yourself up for success by investing in trusted mentors, sponsors, and business coaches. These people should be people you trust with your career and that you know have your best interests at heart. Select people who sing your praises when you are not in the room.

    - My four-legged stool model to build a stable career:

        1. You.

        2. Mentors give you feedback on a specific matter.

        3. Sponsors help you navigate internal politics and are the ones who recommend you for a promotion.

        4. Business coaches are in the trenches with you, see around corners, and help frame your future while holding you accountable every step of the way.

Pay it forward by becoming a mentor and sponsor to other qualified women climbing the ranks.

Have the courage to have faith in yourself. Let it guide you, not make you fearful.

CAREER RESOURCES FROM GAYLE

Don't fall into the trap of complacency. When you are feeling the dullness of working every day or the stress from working with others, consider a retreat to dive deep into reflection on your professional and personal life goals. Being surrounded by like-minded women who empower each other to change and step into their own light is so refreshing and encouraging, and a retreat can be an ideal place to recharge with good food, great exercise, and people who have wonderful ideas. As Chief Reinvention Officer (CRO) of Gayle Keller LLC, I offer retreats and masterminds for women in S.T.E.A.M. that focus on both professional and personal reflection and taking action, where women are surrounded by like-minded and motivated women. To learn more, sign up at https://www.gaylekeller.org

PILLAR 3: CONFIDENCE

ELAINE, THE CONFIDENT ENGINEER

"C'mon, Sweetie. Let's get your coat on. Mommy gets to work today," Elaine said as she handed a fluffy pink coat to her three-year-old daughter.

"Okay, Mommy. I get to go to preschool today, too. We are going to color animals."

"That sounds like a lovely day. I get to draw shopping stores."

Elaine walked into the office and headed to her desk.

"I wish I could come into work fifteen minutes late every day," whispered her colleague, Monique. Fortunately, Elaine didn't hear her.

"Me, too. And I'd like a few days off every month, too," Anita declared.

"Seriously. It must be nice to have special privileges." Monique carried on. "She's not the only one with three kids at home."

"Plus, she has a husband; some of us don't," exclaimed Anita.

"I'm so sorry to keep you all waiting. What did I miss yesterday?" Elaine rushed into the conference room to meet Monique, the Team Facilitator, and Anita, the Junior Project Manager.

"Oh, you know, thirty calls, twenty new files, five data reports, and the survey for the shopping development in Cedar Creek." Monique tried to not sound annoyed. "Here are your files. Sorry we couldn't get to them."

"It is so hard to keep up," Elaine shared. "I'm really trying to make it all work. Where's Pandeep?"

"He's meeting with the Cedar Creek Development Committee, remember? A reminder email and text went out today."

"I haven't had a chance to check my phone. Thanks."

For eleven years, Elaine earned her way to Managing Engineer. She was a high performer who excelled at building teams and managing high demand community development projects. The firm had four levels of management which ensured employee retention. It was a good firm to work with despite the lack of gender diversity, which is the issue with every area of the S.T.E.A.M. industry.

She moved into the role after returning from maternity leave two years ago. Olivia was her third child, preceded by her brother Vincent, who was six, and her sister Julinda, five. Both Vincent and Julinda were in school full-time, while three-year old Olivia was in part-time preschool and cared for by their nanny, Sylvie. Their family would never survive without Sylvie, who cared for the kids, cooked, cleaned, did laundry, ran errands, and even took her mother-in-law to doctor's appointments when needed. Oh, and the guinea pig, Turmeric, needed to be fed three times a day and given free-range time while the cage was being cleaned. Sylvie was Elaine's mini-me. After six years, they had become the kind of close friends that are able to finish each other's sentences.

The team ran through their current projects, closed two that were finished, and reviewed incoming projects. Monique and Anita were new to Elaine's team of ten. With everything going on in Elaine's personal life and the influx of projects as spring approached, there wasn't any time for everyone to get to know each other. Both women were qualified and good at their job, but they were not yet gelling well as a team. When two people who have worked together for years are brought into a new team at a different company, silos are built, and they assume the role of the "outsiders." Never a pleasant feeling for them, and similarly difficult for their manager. It didn't help that Elaine couldn't carve out the time needed to get to know them at present. In time, hopefully, the disconnects between old and new teammates would smooth out.

Elaine stopped in the restroom on her way back to her office, then grabbed a cup of hot tea and filled her water bottle. It had been a semi-stressful morning for a Monday. Sylvie had driven Vincent and Julinda to school for their early art breakthrough class, which left her to have some one-on-one time with Olivia getting her ready for school. She loved spending time with the kids, together and individually. It was such a treasure. Hectic, though. Thank God for messy bun trends. Her shoulder length dark blonde hair had seen hundreds of styles over her lifetime, and, as a working mom of three, the messy bun had been a mainstay, unless she met with a client. Then she wore it in a smoothed, low-hanging ponytail. At least her makeup was on point every day.

"Elaine," Pandeep abruptly called to her, following her into her office.

Startled, Elaine almost spilled her coffee on her desk, near her laptop. "Pandeep, are you trying to give me a heart attack?"

"No, why didn't you get your workout in today?"

"Yes, I did, at 4:30am. It was leg day."

"Oh good, then your heart is still ticking—you are in good shape," Pandeep chuckled.

"Not really. It's been a hectic morning. I drove Olivia to school and had an IVF appointment."

"How did it go yesterday?"

"As well as could be expected. You would never believe the pain. I should be used to it by now, being that we are going for number four. Sometimes, I wonder how I'm going to survive being pregnant, a mom of three, and managing this team and these projects. Plus, it's spring. Have you seen the paperwork? Have you seen the lineup of meetings? On top of that, I feel absolutely awful that Anita and Monique have not been officially welcomed and integrated into the team."

"You need to get that taken care of, Elaine," Pandeep said sternly, his voice lowered. "Team building is an essential stepping stone to the next level in management."

"I know. I know. I'm working on it. Okay, so where is our agenda?" She rifled through papers, looking for it. "I don't understand why, in this world of computers and tech, we need to print everything. Doesn't that seem almost sacrilegious to the environment?"

"Here's today's agenda, Elaine."

"You're a lifesaver. Thanks."

Pandeep and Elaine had been co-leaders of the same team a few years ago, and now Pandeep was at Level 3 Management. Elaine hoped to reach that same rank before her next baby was born. It was different having him as her manager, but they acted more like they were in a mentor-mentee relationship. Pandeep knew about everything that was going on in her work and home life, so the fact that it was slow going with Monique and Anita was understandable. However, he was her boss, and he had to gently move her forward over the last few months as her performance had been waning. Now, as it was the busy season, she needed to step up—or she wouldn't be able to keep up.

"This month's challenges. When aren't there challenges? The first will be to get my desk in order. I need a Sylvie for my office," Elaine laughed.

"Does she do office calls? I could benefit greatly from Sylvie."

"Not yet!" They both laughed.

"Back to challenges. This workload is insane. May I vent?"

Pandeep nodded. Their arrangement when neither was looking for feedback or to solve it, they asked each other about venting just to get it off their minds. Vent, release, and forget about it. It was the best part of their relationship.

"I have ten people working for me with an average of seven projects each. Plus, William is traveling three weeks of the month. With my IVF appointments and embryo implantation in the coming weeks, I'm going to lose more work time. It's so much; I really can't take it."

"You are going to either laugh or hate me." Pandeep said, smiling.

"Why?"

"I just read this article that said white women are the biggest complainers in the job market."

"Whaaaatttt? What does that mean? Where did the study come from?"

"One of the big medical universities studied the most diverse workplaces to identify causes of loss of productivity. They were surprised to find out how much white women complain about their work, while women of other cultures put their heads down and do the same work with few complaints."

"Are you saying I complain too much? I thought we had venting rules."

"We definitely have a special relationship, and venting rules stay. But you need to watch how much you complain and express your frustration. There are new ears on your team, and there's a little chatter going on."

"Thanks for the heads up. I'm grateful you have my back. I'll definitely turn it around. For the next 30 days, I'll be late on Mondays, Wednesdays, and Fridays, including two weeks after the implantation. Can you cover me?"

"Yep, you bet. I just want credit as your work baby daddy. I feel that I contributed to this one the most. Can you name him or her after me?"

Elaine laughed out loud. "Work baby daddy? That's funny. And, we've already picked out names. I'm so sorry."

"It was worth a shot. Good luck this week. Get your team integrated."

"Maybe you could take Family Medical Leave, Elaine," William encouraged. He was at the airport, waiting for his flight to board.

"I don't know, William. Does that make sense? I mean, we'll know in five weeks if this embryo transfer was successful. If it's not, I can rebound fine."

"You've been stressed and behind for several months now while we've gone through this process. You know how they say stress can prevent successful fertilization and implantation."

"That's true. Maybe I should consider something else. What would you say about me going part-time or just staying home?"

"You've worked so hard, Elaine, to get where you are. I would hate to see you leave or switch jobs. Are they even offering part-time? Plus, I think you will be really bored staying home. My sister hated it."

"I know. I just don't think the stress I'm under is good for any of us, especially me. With spring coming, my company has 110 projects we are onboarding. My team is supposed to get 23 of them. That's a lot to juggle. And I have some squawkers that just came onto my team chatting about how I'm late, take off work, and complain about the workload. Maybe they are right."

"It's definitely something to explore," William said supportively. "Gotta board now. Love you."

"Love you, too. Safe travels."

Do I complain too much? Elaine pondered while she jogged on the elliptical. *Do white women complain more than anyone else? Did they do the same study for men? Why would anyone think to conduct such a study? My two newbies are chatting. That is always a bad sign, and clearly, they do not appreciate my complaining. Why am I complaining so much? Have I always been like this? Is it the hormones? Why do we always go to the hormones? They get a bad rap.*

Maybe I should have left during the "Great Resignation" movement like Shelly and Danica did. Where would I be now?

No. I didn't want that. If I'm honest with myself, I can't stand this team. I'm not really excited about integrating them, and now that they've been complaining? I really don't want to have anything to do with them.

I'm also tired of the men in the boardroom complaining and not taking action on anything. Every week, we talk about the same issues, and no one does anything. We need a woman at the top, just like we need women priests and women presidents. We know how to get stuff done. Except, maybe not right now, today, for me.

Ugh. I'm usually so confident; it's what propelled me into engineering. Why is everything so different? I'm not even considering the newbies' feelings, which is so unlike me.

"I did not realize how much differently I'm feeling about working and maybe staying home. Wait. Did I say that out loud? No! William is right. I would hate it. His sister and I are cut from the same cloth. As high performers and achievers, we were both fast-tracked to promotions. It took my friends a lot of courage to leave. I don't want to leave. I love the money, the stock, and the lifestyle. Leaving is not an option, and I can't rock the boat. I'm staying for now, and I'll consider the

FMLA." Elaine commented to herself as she wiped off her forehead, neck, and handlebars.

"That was a good workout. I feel better already."

Exercise always seemed to bring some stability and clarity to Elaine's emotions.

"Okay, we have some special announcements," the CEO announced as everyone gathered around the table. Some leaned against the wall, drinking their coffee or eating their morning bagel. Some scrambled to chairs.

"The engineering firm across town is closing in 30 days. We do not know the details. All we know is that they are forwarding all of their clients to us in seven days. That will double our workload, so in addition to our start teams here, we need to hire more people to support the teams we have in place, plus add on a couple of new leveled managers. We will be conducting interviews for their employees starting tomorrow. We will have individual discussions with anyone who expresses interest or is scheduled for your next tiered position. We hope to have everyone in place in two weeks."

The board members mumbled amongst themselves, sharing whether they were in favor of it or against it or worried about it. Elaine shrunk in her chair, unable to share her thoughts. She really wanted to run out of the room. Her stomach churned.

There's an opening for a Level 3 Manager now*!?! Timing couldn't be worse! There is no way I'll get through spring with more team members and more projects,* she thought to herself. *I'm barely hanging on now with what I have. Why didn't I leave with the girls?*

"Have you talked with Pandeep yet?" Shelly asked.

"No. I just feel so scatterbrained. I wasn't expecting to feel these mixed emotions and so much frustration about the workload. It feels so unnatural for me because I've always been so driven and ready to take on more work. What is wrong with me?"

"Nothing is wrong with you. Nothing at all. You are getting ready to have your fourth baby. You've always had so much on your plate, with a husband that travels for work, your three kids, and the fact you are going for another round of IVF. That alone is challenging, and that's without even considering your career, the team you lead, and all the projects you're juggling. Honestly, I think all women who have families experience this at some point in their career. They said we can do it all, but do we want to? And if we want to, should we, if it means sacrificing ourselves? I honestly don't know how some women 'do it all.'"

Shelly was such a good friend. Shelly and Elaine worked together for ten years prior to the "Great Resignation," or as Elaine reframed the trend, the "Great Reinvention." They were both very sensitive, supportive, understanding, and empathetic women who really put people before work. Overconsumed as Elaine was with her own myriad happenings, she nearly forgot about taking time to nurture her growing team.

"Now that you list everything I have going on right now, it does sound like a lot. I feel like I'm a steam engine just trying to roll over everything to get the next task checked off my list. My poor team. My poor kids. It's not fair to them. Poor me. Do you know when my last yoga session was? I don't even remember. My whole body hurts right now. What should I do, Shelly?"

"I definitely think you need to get to yoga, and you need to get your thoughts organized for a talk with Pandeep."

"You are absolutely right. That is a good plan. I'll ask Sylvie to stay the night and care for the kids. William will be home in the morning. I'm going to go to yoga, journal at the Tea Spot, meditate, and then take a nice long soak in the tub after a quick session of Tai Chi. Thank you for letting me talk through these feelings and my options, Shelly."

"You definitely seem a lot calmer than when we first started talking. Yikes, it's been an hour and twenty-three minutes. I have to grab dinner. Enjoy your evening, Elaine. This is all going to work out; I can feel it."

As they hung up their phones, Elaine pondered, *What am I going to do? God, Universe, Higher Power, I'll need your help on this one!*

"Knock. Knock." Pandeep stood outside Elaine's office.

"Oh! Ouch. You did it again, Pandeep! C'mon in." Elaine said as she looked up from the file. She chuckled as she rubbed the crick in her neck. "What's up? What can I do for you today?"

"I was in the neighborhood and thought I'd say 'hi,'" he said as he walked in, closed the door behind him, and sat down in the office chair on the other side of Elaine's desk, facing her.

"What is it?" Elaine asked as she raised her eyebrows at him, wondering why he shut the door.

"How are you, Elaine? Did you have a nice weekend?"

"Yeah. It was good. Yours?"

"Good. Mine was good, too. Well, I wanted to check in on you. But before I say anything, I want you to know that I'm here as a friend because that means more to me than being your manager. So, when I ask, I want you to be totally honest with me and know that my management hat is back in my office."

Her eyebrows furrowed, Elaine asked, "Of course, I can be totally honest with you. It's a deal. What's going on?"

"During the board meeting, when Miguel announced the new projects and people, I looked at you, and you didn't look happy about it," Pandeep shared cautiously.

"You saw that? I'm so sorry. I was just surprised at the extra work load I would have, and I was hoping to just have a steady and reasonable pace for the next few weeks."

"I know. No worries! We are all good. In fact, I thought about you over much of the weekend, wondering how you could just take it easy for the next few weeks." Pandeep said.

"I'm so glad you are bringing this up, Pandeep. I planned to talk with you today. Thank you for being such a wonderful friend. I am really stressed about the incoming deluge of projects. The timing isn't exactly ideal for me, and I was actually thinking about downshifting a bit until we get through the embryo transfer."

"What did you have in mind?" Pandeep leaned forward out of concern. Elaine realized how much he really cared.

"I was wondering about going on FMLA for a couple of months."

"Hmmm. Mmmm," Pandeep nodded in agreement.

"Then, with the announcement, I evaluated my team, my project load, my schedule, my doctor's appointments, my family commitments, and it all seemed completely overwhelming.

I'm just not sure how I will sustain this role with even more work added onto our plates."

"I completely understand, and that's why I'm here."

"Pandeep, do you know of any opportunities for part-time roles that I could fill for a couple of years or so? Then, I could maybe come back to work full-time in this role when life settles down a bit?"

"I can definitely look into it and get back to you. So, are you thinking about FMLA for the full twelve weeks and then coming back part-time?"

"Well, I hadn't thought it all the way through yet, but yes, I think that sounds really good."

"Let me look into it and get back to you, Elaine."

"Thank you so much, Pandeep. I appreciate you wearing the 'friend with employee benefits' hat to this conversation! I already feel better."

"As much as I would hate to lose you on my team, I really want what's best for you and what keeps you around. Honestly, as your manager, I can't think of a better time for this type of transition. I would rather it happen before we assign the new people and workloads than you think of it after. Hopefully, we can get a win-win out of this!"

"William, I'm so glad you're home. Just in time, too. Pandeep just sent me an offer for a part-time role, and the FMLA papers!"

"That's fantastic, Elaine. I would love for you to have a few months off while we do this IVF cycle. I can't think of a healthier way for you to prepare," William said as he hugged Elaine.

"Timing is everything. You are not going to believe this! Our philanthropy division was getting ready to post a part-time position to lead the projects for the American Heart Association. I asked them if they would consider supporting Mercy Home, too, and they said they would! They want me to head up a team that will double our philanthropic contributions in three years!"

William spun around and gave a joyful shout. "When does FMLA start?"

"Friday is my last day with my team. I don't have to transition my team since the next group is already going to be reassigned with the new workloads. They will divide my team among the new line of managers, so it's all taken care of. I just have to sign the FMLA papers, meet my new supervisor, pack up my office, and come home for twelve blissful weeks!"

"What are you going to do first?" William asked after they embraced and shouted for joy.

"I'm going to take a long bubble bath and finally finish reading *How to Raise Successful People* by Esther Wojcicki. I started it a year ago. What do you think the kids will say?"

They both laughed out loud. It wasn't a stretch to predict that the kids would be ecstatic to be spending more time with their mom.

This life-shift is going to be different, and we are going to relish every minute together. It's quite nice to know it can work out so well for all of us, Elaine thought to herself as she smiled and hugged William tighter.

ELAINE'S REFLECTION & PLAN TO CALL UP SELF-CONFIDENCE & GET WHAT SHE WANTS

STEP 1 - AWARENESS

What was the situation?

Before she had kids, Elaine was a well-regarded superstar at her office. In her reviews, she was placed on the fast-track, which meant higher salary increases and quicker promotions. In ten years, she received six promotions to middle management, and had one more to go to reach Pandeep's level. She kept the pace at work even after having her first two kids. When the third one came, she slowed down quite a bit, and no longer had time to work from her laptop at night and get ahead for the next day. Work had to stay at work, and her home life at home. Occasionally, if the dinner and bedtime routines went smoothly, she used her phone to plan for the day.

With the recent announcement from the board about the new projects and staff, her heart sank to her stomach. That was the red flag that surprised her the most. She normally would be vying for the most projects and the most qualified team members to win the year-end achievement awards.

This time, she immediately felt dread. Added stress rose up in her, which immediately led her to become worried about the outcome of the scheduled embryo implantation. That was the turning point. She had never felt that. It was time for a change.

She treasured evenings with her little ones, especially reading time. They snuggled, giggled, and took turns reading the pages and making funny voices to bring the story to life. As much as she loved her career, some days it was hard to decide what she should prioritize—work or kids. Without a doubt, her family was the most important element of her life. She and William wanted a big family. On the mornings when laughter and hugs filled the kitchen, she sometimes felt a pang about working that day. A fleeting thought crept into her mind as she wondered what it would be like to stay home with them for the day. But then, the bus honked. Sylvie put their coats on, and Elaine rushed to tie shoes and zip up boots. Before she could even seriously consider it, she was in the car, headed to the office.

Three kids outnumbered her, William, and Sylvie at any given moment. *How would it work with the fourth baby? It's a lot.*

As she dreamed about the fourth baby—boy or girl—and how they would all love the baby, she thought, *Stress can't be part of this procedure. I really need to be 100% ready and relaxed for it.*

Yoga was, as always, centering, clearing, and fulfilling. At the Tea Spot, Elaine ordered the green ginger blend with a mixed vegetable cup and headed to the table with the nicest view. Elaine encouraged herself, "Okay, girl, you've got to figure this out. What is in your heart? Make sure you pay attention to your instincts and gut while you journal. Listen to the whispers."

How was it affecting others?

Work. Her team was chattering about her being late and taking time off. They did not know she was going through fertility treatments. She was losing her stellar reputation, and that hurt. She also felt behind every day and knew she wasn't pulling all the weight she once had for her team, and that she was not functioning at the 110% level that she expected from herself. If Elaine changed roles, she changed teams, which meant she would not report to Pandeep. It was a big shift.

Family & Friends. Staying home or working in a part-time position would afford Elaine more family time with William, their kids, her parents, and her friends, which would be especially helpful as William's travel had increased significantly. Maybe they could sneak away on a couple's retreat. The kids would love seeing Elaine more, and Elaine would love that, too.

Elaine. Always a high-achiever, Elaine operated on all cylinders at all times until their third child, and something shifted. Her lackluster energy could be caused by lack of sleep, too much on her plate, hormones, aging; anything, really. All she knew was that her tank was always only half full. A lighter workload meant less stress and more family time, which meant she could carve out some time for herself. Whenever she had her own time, she returned a better mother, wife, daughter, friend, and woman.

STEP 2 - OPTIONS

Elaine's ultimate goal was to obtain a part-time role for the next several years until all the kids were in school full-time. That way, she could live with better work-life balance for work and her family. She wrote out all of her options.

1. A promotion to Level 3 Manager with the new clients and team members was a possible path, but Elaine felt her eyes glaze over just thinking about it. So, it really wasn't an option.

2. If she stayed in her current role, she could take family medical leave, then request a middle manager role or part-time position when she returned.

3. She could look into opportunities for a part-time position; that sounded like the best option so far.

4. She considered what staying at home would look like, and, being honest with herself, it made her a little nervous because there would be a lack of stimulation and contact with adults comparable to what she has at her place of work in the present.

STEP 3 – RISK v. REWARD

There are risks and rewards to every action we take or don't take.

Elaine's physical, emotional, mental, and spiritual health were already drained from the grind of her responsibilities at work and at home. Given her options, which decision would give her time to focus on herself?

With career, family, and personal needs, one of the first things to go in Elaine's life was usually exercise and healthy eating. These were important parts of her daily life; exercise is the antidote to stress and mental health issues. However, this year had been extremely stressful, and it seemed like exercise wasn't enough some days.

Fortunately, having Sylvie as part of the family allowed Elaine and William the time to care for their physical health in their home gym. Sylvie was an avid cook of healthy foods, ensuring all the required food groups were represented in each meal. They were well taken care of and considered themselves to be a healthy, active family. The family would also often take a walk after dinner when the weather was nice.

Where was the time in their day when they could practice their spirituality?

Elaine and William practiced their faith regularly, and all the kids were baptized Catholic. In her early thirties, Elaine preferred more connection and started yoga, chakra work, and more metaphysical practices, which she considered additions to her main faith. Her spirit told her that any connection to God is a good connection when the heart is pure.

Unfortunately, like exercise, spirituality had to be worked at, and when it wasn't, it waned. A life without faith of any kind seemed to leave Elaine feeling without purpose.

However, when she practiced her faith regularly and included it in everyday practices, her mood was elevated, challenges were easier to survive, and clarity of purpose was present in her life. Elaine loved sharing her faith with her kids, and they were so sweet as they accepted faith as an important part of their life. Each night after reading time, Elaine read a short prayer for them at the end of their beds. It was an important part of life that she wanted to instill in their daily lives, because faith is for all times in life.

Which career decision would best support her family's financial goals?

Financially, Elaine and William were in good shape. They had two separate incomes for 15 years, and their 401Ks were built over that time, so they were ahead for retirement. They lived in a modest home surrounded by much larger homes, as they never wanted to live beyond their means. They began saving for the kids' college funds as soon as their first son, Vincent, was born. Technically, they would be able to live solely on William's income even if Elaine opted to stay home full-time.

However, changing her job to part-time would most likely take her out of an engineering role, which she loved, and the pay cut would be significant. Staying home full-time would lead to them not feeling as financially secure as they feel now. Plus, Elaine didn't know if staying home full-time would allow her to satisfy her professional drive.

If she could find a part-time position, she was hopeful for a job with less stress than her current role where she could earn a significant enough income to stay financially on track.

STEP 4 – APPROACH

What was the best approach?

1. **Decide with William.** Willian and Elaine talked, and Elaine sort of agreed with him that staying at home might drive her bananas. If there weren't any part-time positions, though, then there wouldn't be a choice. She couldn't really look for a part-time job elsewhere, because the fertility treatments and hopeful pregnancy were covered by her benefits.

2. **Talk with Pandeep.** Elaine was curious about Pandeep's thoughts after the vent session. Elaine asked if he knew of any part-time roles available in the company.

3. **Evaluate options to make the best decision for her family.** Elaine had a lot to consider.

STEP 5 – AGENT FOR CHANGE

Big Shift. Facing the truth that she couldn't perform at her optimum level at work and home was a big shift for Elaine. She was still Wonder Woman in all areas of her life. Varying obligations require different amounts of time. She refused to feel less than or like a failure because she knew her capabilities and her choices were focused on what made her happiest and helped her feel the most fulfilled.

Intellectual Stimulation. The advantages to having a career while raising a family are the brain stimulation and the social aspects work provides. Eileen knew she would be a little bored if a part-time job wasn't available, though she knew that lots of volunteer opportunities would be available to her if she needed them. She also knew that the kids needed their brains stimulated as well, and she would definitely be a part of that, too.

Highest Priority. When she thought of her priorities and how she wanted her life to look, she wanted family to come first. Her oldest was already reaching school age, and she and William wanted to have a couple of more kids, God willing. Elaine saw herself at the center of all of it. Part-time work and home would be her first choice. However, if it came down to it, she would stay home full-time. If she had extra ambition or energy, she could volunteer at church and other organizations when she was available.

GAYLE'S REFLECTIONS ON STEPPING INTO YOUR CONFIDENCE

Juggling all of our responsibilities is physically exhausting and emotionally taxing. As a working mom, it is a challenge to be great at everything. We must have the confidence in ourselves to balance our priorities and ask for help when we need it from our colleagues, managers, families, and partners.

It takes a village to raise a child. With that said, it is vital to balance our priorities and pivot when necessary. Elaine took accountability into her own hands, evaluating what is working in her career and what is not so she can stay focused on her top priority: her family.

Like life, careers are not formed in a linear fashion throughout our many seasons of life. There are twists, turns, pivots, challenges we weather, and celebrations, the outcomes of these we weigh so we can confidently lead with our best foot forward. I'm not saying these are easy to address, diagnose, or solve. What I am saying is "be brave and reevaluate your priorities and goals when necessary."

Taking the time to plan your career and establish your goals will not only make you a better person, but also a better role model for your children. Setting boundaries and saying no (or saying "no, not right now") to something you would otherwise love to say "yes" to is essential as well. It's never easy to say "no" to something that tugs at your heartstrings. That's why it's key to have a trusted circle of people in your life that will hold you authentically accountable.

GAYLE'S PRESCRIPTION TO OWNING YOUR CONFIDENCE

It's important to give yourself grace throughout your many seasons of life. Here are some considerations to take into account when you look to make a change in your life.

1. Exercise grit and leverage a strong work ethic.

2. Be coachable with your managers, mentors, and sponsors, and be open to feedback. Feedback is not negative; it's a way to sharpen your skill sets and strengths, and also improve your weaknesses.

3. We live in a work / life integrated world, and it's imperative to set boundaries and prioritize what is important to you—both at home and the workplace.

4. Do not be afraid to be wrong. Learn from your mistakes, failures, and losses, and only try to make improvements once you understand how to do things differently the next time around.

5. Be respectfully curious and assertive in the workplace. Do not pass judgment. When in doubt, ask for clarification and listen with intent.

CAREER RESOURCES FROM GAYLE

As a podcast host for Theodora Speaks™, I learn from and am inspired by the guests I'm honored to interview. In S2:E20 - "Encouraging Equality," Alison McConnell, CMO of Publicis Health Media, shares her recipe for balance. Like Elaine, McConnell is a working mom who encourages us to ask for what we want in our careers. Not only that, she encourages and empowers brands to reimagine gender inclusion, equity, equality, and diversity.

There are so many recommended episodes to tune into that give tangible tools to implement in our lives. Another recommended episode is S1:E08 - "One Good [Engineering] Woman" with Cheryl Maletich, Senior Vice President of Transmission and Substation at ComEd, a unit of Chicago-based Exelon Corporation (a Fortune 100 energy company), who shares tenacious tales from her experiences as an engineer. Leadership comes naturally to Cheryl, as does her ability to support other women as they climb the ranks. She emphasizes the significance of giving back and how philanthropic work fuels her soul. Cheryl is a firm believer in "how you act when you fail says as much about you as when you succeed."

Theodora Speaks™ on Apple Podcasts: https://podcasts.apple.com/us/podcast/theodora-speaks/id1555760344

PILLAR 4: COURAGE

ANTONIA, THE COURAGEOUS ARTIST

"...And the #MeToo movement opened the doors for all of us to stand up for ourselves. Have we? Are we? Will we? Friends, sexual harassment has no boundaries when it comes to age, gender, sexual orientation, race, or profession. So if it has happened, is happening, or will happen, do we know exactly what it looks like and how to stand up for ourselves?"

This speaker is good, Antonia thought to herself. *It's true. I don't think many of my friends would recognize or admit that a little flirting at the office can lead to sexual harassment because of the mixed signals we give. Sometimes, we don't even know we are flirting.*

"... Stand up, stand up," the speaker was saying.

Everyone is standing up. ¡Ay, caramba! I have to pay attention. Antonia shook herself out of her daydream.

"This is my favorite pose because it makes me feel powerful and gives me enough courage to handle anything. Let's do this together.

"Stand tall.

"Put your hands on your hips with your fingers facing forward, so the sides of your palms are parallel to the ground.

"Separate your legs to a little more than a shoulder's width apart.

"Look up at the ceiling.

"Big, deep breath in.

"Big, slow exhale out as you tilt your head back.

"Ahhhh.

"Now we are in our power stance. Does it remind you of Wonder Woman? Yeah, she had it figured out. And that is who we are. Wonder Women. Wonder Men."

The speaker crossed her wrists together.

"Oh wow!" Antonia exclaimed. She leaned over to Sarah. "Sarah, she has the Wonder Women cuffs on!"

"The what?"

"Her wrist cuffs. You know, the gold ones I saw at the store and started saving for?"

"Yeah. Yeah. I remember. That's kinda cool," Sarah said, halfway in a daze, as she was very focused on her inhale and exhale.

We both hung onto Theordora's every word. She had spoken to this group before, and had been well received both times.

"Any time you find yourself in an unusual predicament, pull out your Wonder Woman self and power up."

"She really is my hero. I really like this speaker. What she said makes sense, and I know I can remember it and apply it," Sarah said to Antonia.

"Yeah, me too. She's made me question how I used to handle uncomfortable situations."

The speaker wrapped up while they were still standing in their power pose.

"Well, that's one way to get a standing ovation," Antonia chuckled. "Close it out while everyone stands for the last exercise."

"Kinda brilliant, if you ask me," Sarah mentioned.

"For sure," Antonia agreed. "What's her name, again?"

"Thea. Ummm. Theodora."

Buzzzzzz. The alarm clock sounded. She slapped around for the alarm clock and finally hit the right button, shutting off the blaring noise.

"Ugh. Coffee. I need coffee," she said, trying to remember which day it was and whether she had to get up or could hit the snooze button.

Monday! It's prepping day! I love Mondays! But where did the weekend go—how did it go by so quickly? Oh... We saw that speaker on Saturday. Her presentation was about sexual harassment in the workplace, Antonia's mind raced as she pulled herself out of bed and started her morning routine. *Yeah, sexual harassment. I guess I can relate to it.*

Much of what the speaker had talked about was happening to Antonia now. So far, she had brushed it off as innocent flirting that sometimes went a bit too far, but it was getting to be awkward and uncomfortable. *It was a good way to spend a Saturday with Sarah. I learned a lot.*

Antonia rubbed her eyes, gently slapped her cheeks, rolled out of bed, put on some fleece pants, her fuzzy slippers, and a sweatshirt from her alma mater.

"Yay. Planning day. All the comfy feels. No calls. Just creative planning and prepping for this week's projects."

As she beelined for the coffee maker, she stopped to sprinkle fish food into her 30-gallon aquarium that was centrally located between the dining room and the living room of her home, a duplex in a modern subdivision. Antonia loved color in her life. Her aquarium was home to several saltwater fish she had collected over the years, once she had the means to support herself fully and independently.

Since Antonia was a little girl, she had been mesmerized by fish, their smooth swimming and the subtle movements of their fins as they navigated their paths through the water. The vibrant and sometimes neon colors inspired her to think outside of the box, which enhanced her creativity as a sculpture artist and jewelry maker. The patterns in which the fish swam on occasion resembled the curvature of some rings, cuffs, and other such adornments, and the colors of the fish were the baseline for the color schemes she pulled together for some of her jewelry. The colors were fresh and complex, not at all the common tones one would see in the typical jewelry piece or sculpture.

In keeping with the most popular denizens of others' freshwater aquariums, Antonia had purchased an orange, white, and black clownfish she'd named "Nemo," after the titular character of the Disney movie. Her Green Chromis fish is a blend of neon blue, green, and yellow, and its scales shimmer in different lights. A BiColor Blenny holds the award for two-tone with its purplish-blue and orange colorings. The Firefish Goby is white with red fins at the end, and a black stripe on its tail fin.

They were fun for Antonia to watch. She loved when they chased each other. She also loved that there wasn't a mess to clean up, since she had the 'aquarium guy' come over weekly to service the tank.

Her life as an acclaimed artist needed simplicity at all times because she could be commissioned to carve a sculpture at any given moment. A travel suitcase with five days' worth of supplies was at the ready whenever a call came. She traveled about fifteen days out of every month and worked all over the world.

She was recognized as a talented artist when she was younger. Her high school art teacher commissioned her and three other art students to create a graffiti mural. It had been the first time she sketched and painted a mural. She liked it quite a lot, but when the class switched to metallurgy and they made jewelry and steel sculptures, she put her paintbrushes away for a while and focused on learning the look, weight, and feel of various metals, as well as the elements that comprised them. It was the beginning of her love of metals, sculpting, and art: the perfect blend of her three favorite topics. Working with metals required art, science, and math. She took a jewelry making class or two on the weekend, which expanded her artistic talents and created opportunities for her to give back to her two favorite nonprofit organizations.

Antonia's mom was the regional director for the Susan G. Komen 30-mile walk to fight breast cancer. To raise money, Antonia had been asked to make special necklaces for each of the teams. It took six months to make them, as she worked on them after school and after doing her homework, but it had been a special honor. The director honored Antonia on stage for the creative talents she shared with them for their fundraiser. The profits made from selling her jewelry made up $12,000 of the total money raised. After word spread about Antonia's necklace fundraiser, the Alzheimer's Association where she and her Papi volunteered every quarter commissioned her to create a special coin, one showing the brain with a heart. It was the perfect special project for her, as she blended jewels with melted metals to create a colorful momento for their donors.

In high school, soccer was Antonia's favorite sport and only activity after school. However, what she most loved to do was to watch her Papi carve wood sculptures from tree trunks. He used tree trunks that he brought home after a client's tree removal job. Using his forestry education, he had branched out on his own shortly after college and built his own tree care company. He dabbled in art and had a second revenue stream from selling his wooden carvings and wood sculptures. He sculpted at least five pieces a week, and had a six-month waitlist at all times for his works until he retired.

As soon as Mamacita heard Antonia's laughter and fast talking, she would bring out a tray of fruit, cheese, and crackers, as well as tall glasses of water and a little piece of chocolate. After they caught up on the day, they had dinner together at the table, continued their conversation, and then had individual family time. Papi read the day's newspaper, Mami crocheted or planned the next day, and Antonia watched Wonder Woman or read her book for the week. That particular week she was reading *The Leadership Renaissance: Blending the Art and Science of You in Five Simple Steps* by Teri Goudie, Dave Heilmann, Jim Hutchinson, and Caylen Bufalino. She appreciated the authors' insight about storytelling being the most important element to interweave into everything a person creates. She had always been complimented on how people feel the story of her sculptures and how it moves their hearts.

Antonia loved the process of carving. When she watched her dad, his first step was to carve a large oval shape, like a head, if he was doing a bust. Then, he carved the more prominent features, like hair, cheekbones, chin, nose, and ears. Lastly, he finished the finer details, like eyebrows, lips, eyelashes, and laugh lines. Watching him work so deliberately with his hands on the chisel was a gift to Antonia. He had such finesse and attention to detail. At times, he became "one with the tree," and, other times, it seemed he and the tree trunk would get annoyed at each other.

All good artists clash with their projects from time to time. Antonia had a love-hate relationship with a few of her sculptures that were in the big government centers. Most of the time, aggravation abounded when the metal was impacted by the weather and wouldn't bend as smoothly as she preferred. Like all worthwhile endeavors, it took time, and, more often than not, she would eventually win out over the stubbornness of the metal. She was stubborn, feisty, creative, crafty, frugal, athletic, independent, in-tune, and innovative. These traits were what her clients liked best about her, though they especially appreciated how her cost-conscious nature did not compromise the integrity or quality of her work.

Her recently commissioned project required her to spend Tuesday through Saturday away from home. She would be going to New Orleans to work on a special installment at the

Helis Foundation's Enrique Alferez Sculpture Garden. It was a display in the New Orleans Botanical Garden to celebrate the history, influence, and work of the Mexican-American artist Enrique Alferez. The Garden was to honor his memory and timeless work with a steel sculpture that would serve as protection from bad weather in the outdoor amphitheater. They had various materials shading visitors to the garden, but nothing as impressive as Antonia's plans. Her innovative and extravagant approach was the reason she won the bid.

She was thoroughly enjoying the process and the team assigned to her. However, there was one team member, the supervisor, who seemed to be perturbed by her presence. He made a lot of poor decisions related to her. They both grew up with artistic fathers and they had a lot in common. He didn't seem to like that she was responsible for the final decisions on the sculpture's design and placement. She had grown uncomfortable with his communication style, awkward physical contact, and strange sense of humor that was laden with sexual innuendos.

Antonia didn't think too much about it at first. Some people are born to bring comic relief to certain situations. But his words and behavior went much farther than benign, if tasteless, jokes. She had worked in a male-dominated field long enough to become accustomed to innuendo or straight-out blasphemous acts being treated as laughing matters among her peer group.

When it came to Samuel, though, there just seemed to be something "off" about him. She no longer thought he was just making idle conversation, nor just accidentally disrespecting her boundaries. The red flags in her gut were waving wildly. However, he had been a curator for Helis for a long time, and was also a sculptor of metals and resin. She heard rumblings that he was in line for the installment Antonia won, but they needed him more as a supervisor because he was very good at it. He was well-respected by his peers and team members—who all just so happened to be men.

For a day in New Orleans, it was a bit damp and rainy. As Antonia rushed out the door, she grabbed her hooded sweatshirt, just in case. By the time she arrived on the grounds to continue her work, it was chilly, so she pulled her sweatshirt over her head. She did not like restrictive clothing when sculpting; she needed for her limbs to remain loose and free so she could use her entire body to mold and bend the steel. This particular project required large pieces which required use of her whole body.

The other caveat to wearing loose clothing at work was that it could get stuck in the crevices of her statue or snag on cuts or shards of steel, which could be dangerous to her. This was one reason why she heavily invested in one-piece bodysuits. Similar to diving suits, the one piece lycra bodysuit fit her in a snug way, but it was not provocative. She was an avid health nut and dancer when soccer wasn't in season. Staying in shape was an important benefit of her large-sculpture assignments, which were very taxing on the body. She loved the demand it placed on her muscles because it contributed to her fitness goals.

Antonia stopped by the office to put her lunch in the fridge. She liked to start early, often rising with the sun, as she loved hearing birdsong as she set about her day, preparing her tools and supplies. No one usually came in until later.

"Sweatshirt in New Orleans? You are definitely thin-blooded, Antonia."

"Samuel, good morning! You are here early."

He followed her to the fridge.

"You know, Antonia, I prefer the view from my office when you're not wearing the sweatshirt," Samuel said, as he placed four fingers on her shoulder and slid them down her back as she bent up from the fridge.

"Samuel, I need to work," Antonia jerked away, as she thought, *Dios mio. Now I know I'm not imagining this. That was the most forward he has been.*

All of a sudden, he hit her on her rear.

"What?! Samuel. That is not okay."

"Really, Señorita, not okay? I know you like it. You are far from home, and I'm sure you need a release. You have been so intense lately. When do you make time to play? You know, all work and no play makes a girl's hair very gray," Samuel chortled, watching her facial expressions.

"Um," Antonia started.

"I'm just joking, Antonia! Can't a girl take a joke anymore?" He put his hand around her shoulders, squeezing her closer so her breast touched the side of his torso.

"Eww. That's not appropriate, Samuel," she scolded as she twisted out of his embrace.

"We're just having a little bit of fun. Don't you want to make sure you stay on as our sculptor? You don't want to be known as a troublemaker, do you?" he whispered as he moved closer to her. He was within inches of her face, blocking her path to the door.

"You've been doing a very good job, and everyone is raving about your work. I, personally, think it should have a little more finesse to it, and I know how to move energy through you to get it to be more…"

He waved his hands in the air, one of them landing on the side of her head. He pulled a strand of her hair down alongside her face and twirled it as he searched for the word, then said, "finesse-y."

Antonia yanked her head away so he no longer held her hair. He stepped closer and refused her passage to the door.

"I know how you like tools, Antonia. I see you play with yours. This tool could be all yours, too," he whispered creepily, trying to sound sexy as he massaged the front of his pants. "In fact, you need to decide to play soon, or bad things could start happening."

Ring. Ring.

The door opened, and Dino stepped in. "Good morning, folks! It's gonna be a good day. Not too steamy."

At the sound of the door opening, Samuel jumped back. It was exactly the exit she needed to get out of that situation. Saved by the bell.

Stunned and shaken, Antonia, trying to hide her facial expression, greeted Dino and passed through the door. She needed air. Instead of walking to the garden, she needed time in her car. As she walked to the parking lot, her stomach churned, her head spun, and her hands were shaking.

What just happened? Antonia asked herself, still stunned and still unable to catch her breath. She was enraged. In all the male-dominated spaces she'd been in over 20 years, never had she been treated with such disrespect as a woman as she had been just now.

Her mind raced as she played back the scene. *First of all, he touched me completely inappropriately. The hands down the back, twirling my hair, the slap on my ass? What? And then, if that wasn't enough, a weird hug, encroaching on my personal space within inches, rubbing his—whatever—and then threatening me if I don't 'play.' What am I supposed to do with this?*

What should I do? What can I do? Can I do anything? Antonia's mind raced.

Ok. First, slow down and breathe. She inhaled and exhaled slowly five times until she felt her belly fill up with fresh air without it getting stuck between her throat and abdomen. That was the anxiety talking.

"Now that I'm a bit calmer, I can work through this. What do I do first?

"Let's go through the whole experience since it's fresh in my mind. Ick. I definitely don't want to do this. I could feel his hands on me. It was unsettling, to say the very least."

Antonia decided to document the entire situation while it was still fresh in her mind. She started to type it all into her phone. When she finished, she searched "steps to sexual harassment complaints" on the internet and found the site, "How To Report Sexual Harassment At Work In A Step-By-Step Process."

"I really don't want to file a formal complaint unless I have to. I just want to do my job, but I also don't want this to continue. I'm glad to know the process and that retaliation is illegal. I have the steps. I will email Samuel to hopefully put him on notice and get him to stop the inappropriate behaviors. That will be the first step.

"If he backs off, that's all I will do. If he continues or makes it worse, I will report it and deal with the process. I've always been one to tell myself that if anything happened to me, I would want to be strong for myself and for the women behind me. I guess I'm being called to examine this and take action."

"I am literally a bundle of nerves. Antonia, stop it. Where's your power pose you learned from the speaker. Oh, that's right!" Antonia said to herself. She assumed the pose and took a deep breath: inhale, then exhale. Then, she sat down and wrote the letter.

Samuel,

I'm writing to notify you that I do not appreciate the behavior and actions you are taking with me. They are unwelcome. Since I started working here, there have been several situations where sexual innuendos were directed toward me from you, and you have touched me physically in odd ways. Today was the worst behavior I have ever experienced in my entire life and career. Here is a recount of what happened.

1. I arrived early at 7:30am and stopped by the office to put my lunch in the fridge.

2. You followed me to the fridge, and as I stood back up from putting away my lunch, I felt your hand on my shoulder, which then slid down my back to my hip. You followed this up with the comment that you prefer the view of me from your office when I'm not wearing my sweatshirt.

3. Then, you slapped me on my rear. I immediately told you that behavior was not okay.

4. Your reply was, "We're just having a little bit of fun. Don't you want to make sure you stay on as our

sculptor? You don't want to be known as a troublemaker, do you?" I consider this a threat to my continued employment at the garden.

5. You then blocked my path to the door by invading my private space and standing within inches of my face while you twirled a strand of my hair and whispered about my work needing more "finesse." You then indicated that you know how to increase my energy to elevate my creativity.

6. You mentioned how I play with tools for my project and invited me to play with your "tool," which you indicated by massaging the front of your pants. You said, "This tool could be all yours, too."

7. Then you indicated that if I wasn't up for "playing" (*inferred while mentioning your "tool" and massaging the front of your pants*), then "'bad things' could start happening." Again, I take this as a threat.

8. Fortunately, I was able to leave when Dino came into the office. I had doubts as to whether you would let me leave had he not shown up, which also heightened my discomfort with your actions.

This experience with you left me shaken and stressed. I don't feel comfortable being with you: not in the same room nor in any nearby vicinity. I did not do anything to deserve this treatment, and I did not invite it from you. I'm putting you on notice so that you know that I have documented it. I will continue to document any additional behavior or messages from you that are inappropriate. If another occurrence happens or I am mistreated by you because of this email, I will be submitting it to human resources with a formal sexual harassment complaint against you.

I do not welcome your advances, I do not take kindly to sexual harassment, and I will not put up with threats about my job. You have a lot at stake if a complaint is filed against you. I advise you to keep your interactions with me, and near me, at the highest level of professionalism. Do not touch me in any way, shape, or form again. Or I can guarantee that I will report you.

I look forward to completing this project on time, within budget, in a nonthreatening and professional environment.

Sincerely,

Antonia

Antonia sent the email to Samuel, copying herself so she would have the document on her personal email as well as her professional address. The next time she went into the office, he stayed clear of her and went to another room until she left the building. In Antonia's case, he was threatened by the email. Had he not been, she would have gone through the proper channels to file a formal complaint.

"I'd like to thank Antonia for this exceptional steel sculpture that will shelter our garden-goers during unexpected weather while they are visiting the Helis Garden. Antonia, I am happy to present this award for innovative and purposeful art to you on behalf of the New Orleans Botanical Gardens. Thank you for your unwavering commitment to art."

Samuel shook Antonia's hand, and a golden glimmer caught a few people's eyes. As he gave her the plaque, she assumed her Wonder Woman power pose and held it above her head.

The gold cuff bracelets she wore reflected a shimmering light into the crowd. The crowd roared, offering her a standing ovation. Antonia smiled, feeling satisfaction with her acclaimed art installment, having stood up for herself, and for exhibiting the utmost professionalism in a challenging team environment.

ANTONIA'S REFLECTION & PLAN TO COURAGEOUSLY STAND FOR HERSELF

Antonia desires to encourage us to dig deep for courage when our challenges call for it. Inappropriate behavior and actions in the workplace—or anyplace—are always unacceptable. Through her experience with sexual harassment and sexual advances, she teaches us the steps one needs to take to address such a horrible situation. In Antonia's case, the letter worked, but that won't always be the case. Sometimes courage needs to extend to the next step, which would be filing a formal written complaint. Follow along with Antonia as she shares her decision-making process with you.

STEP 1 – AWARENESS

What was the background of Antonia's situation?

Being in a male-dominated career entails a higher risk for female employees to be subjected to inappropriate talk, chiding, flirting, and sexual advances. While Antonia put up with a lot of the former, the actual, direct sexual comments, advances, and touches were something she had never before experienced. She commanded attention and respect through her stature, reputation, and talent. Most men understood her laser-focus on her work and knew she was professional in every aspect of her projects. Her previous knowledge of such situations was derived from what she had heard on the news and from other friends.

What could she do?

When it happened to her she was stunned, creeped out, and ashamed. She had nothing to be ashamed of—she just felt that way. This is an unfortunately common feeling in response to experiencing sexual misconduct, even though she didn't do anything wrong. She was putting her lunch in the refrigerator, and her project supervisor chose that moment to make serious advances on her. Luckily, she was saved from further discomfort when Dino walked in to clock in. Antonia had to call upon courage in other situations throughout her life. This required a whole different level of courage, and she wanted to find the right path, so she didn't lose the project or get a bad reputation. An online search regarding what she should do to protect herself was the way to go.

How was it affecting others?

Work. The inappropriate talk and behaviors shook Antonia to her core. It was going to be something that caused her nerves and discomfort for a long time. Every time she wore her body suit while she was up on the structure in plain sight of her boss's office window, she would feel the creepy crawlies. It was enough to happen once, but those feelings and emotions don't go away immediately. She would always have to be aware of everyone around her while she was working. What she was more concerned about was how many women and/or men had similar experiences to hers. Was there a list of victims?

Family. Antonia's family would stand behind her 100%. She was not nervous about their reactions, and she knew she would receive their love and support. The idea of this happening to her sweet nieces angered her beyond control. She knew she was strong, but this unwelcome thought gave her enough strength she surmised that she could crush a wind turbine into pieces.

Her. Antonia considered her own self-esteem, the other women at the organization, and her nieces, and knew that she could not just push this under the rug and ignore it. She had to stand up for herself so this didn't happen again—to her or to anyone else.

STEP 2 – OPTIONS

Antonia's ultimate goal was to take action that would stop his behavior without any repercussions to her person, project, or reputation. She knew it would take a lot of courage. Fortunately, she had plenty of that.

After her online research, she learned that she had a few options.

1. **Talk to him directly.** This situation with Samuel had been escalating, and this was the peak of that escalation, so something had to end—this situation couldn't be allowed to happen again.

2. **Abandon the project.** How would that affect Antonia's reputation and portfolio? Antonia built a business and renowned reputation that she isn't going to risk degrading because of this. Not an option.

3. **Report him to Human Resources.** Reporting someone is always daunting, and she didn't have a camera or a witness to prove what happened. It would be her word against his. The threat was of utmost concern to her because he'd said that, "if [Antonia didn't] decide to play soon, bad things could happen..." If she did report him, she would take down the man who helped build the garden and who had worked on it for more than 25 years. He's well respected in many social circles and communities, and if this went to trial, she would never win. Or would she? Have there been other similar complaints about his behavior? Furthermore, would she even necessarily be able to take him to court? Would the company backing him value his skills and seniority over her well-being, and go out of their way to pressure her to settle the matter quietly and take a hit to her own reputation?

STEP 3 – RISK v. REWARD

There are risks and rewards to every action we take or don't take.

If Antonia chose to take a quick break and return to her work without doing anything about Samuel's behavior, what would happen?

Returning to work after a quick break would have potentially given Samuel the impression that she was not affected by the situation, which may lead him to believe that she "liked it." However, she chose to stay on company property because she didn't want to face repercussions, or for someone else to spin a narrative about her behavior because she "left for the day."

If Antonia left work and went home for the day—or longer—what would have been the outcome?

If Antonia left work to go home, she worried that she would show weakness to Samuel by not having the strength to handle the situation. But, what's to handle? It never should have happened. She did not want to give him the impression that she was weak and he could keep harassing her. In addition, if she did leave, he could make up a reason to suspend her or fire her from the project, and she did not want that to happen.

What would happen if she reported it right away?

Antonia was very stressed, emotional, and unsure of what to do. At that moment, and for a while after, she did not have the capacity to control her emotions. If she was going to report it, she preferred to show up as a professional with a well-thought-out plan.

STEP 4 – APPROACH

What was the best approach?

Antonia's work environment and its related stressors would definitely impact her current project, and not in a positive light. The situation must be addressed. Confronting the issue could lead to positive outcomes for her and for other women who may have been affected by Samuel's behavior.

It was time for her to research and identify which steps to take that would result in a better, less emotional conversation. She spent a bit of time searching for possible steps to a solution, returned to work, and thought through her options.

1. **Document the Experience.** Going back to the beginning of the project, Antonia had to remember all the little stuff she endured from Samuel. Each one was a step he tested to get closer to today's incident. Why didn't she cut it off at the forefront instead of letting it slide? What should she have said? Her research said to document every occurrence. She started writing a list.

2. **Email Samuel.** When Antonia Googled "process for sexual harassment complaints," it recommended emailing the harasser, putting them on notice, and demanding they stop the behavior. She wondered if this would be effective enough.

3. **Sit Down with HR to Discuss.** In order to report him, the article highly recommended Antonia sit down with someone from human resources when she wrote the report.

4. **Workplace Retaliation is Illegal.** She found relief in knowing that retaliating was illegal. He already threatened her, but maybe once he received her email, he

would stop. And if she chose to take it to the next level, he could not take her project away or dismiss her. He might make things difficult for her, but she could probably report that, too.

STEP 5 – AGENT FOR CHANGE

Dig Deep for Courage. The research was very helpful, and she felt confident she would find the courage to stand up for herself.

Tone. Antonia knew that there was not going to be a second chance to set the right tone, and she did not want it to be friendly or joking. She vowed to herself that her decision would be firm and serious.

Desired Outcome. While that uncomfortable day was more than anything she could or wanted to handle, and she had a case that she could report, she did not want to take that step yet. She didn't have long to complete her project, and she just wanted to be effective in getting him to stop.

Resources. With the research she did, she decided she was most comfortable with her first step being to write a letter to him, demanding he stop the behavior immediately or a report would be written.

GAYLE'S REFLECTIONS ON COURAGE

Sexual harassment and gender biases are not acceptable, especially in the workplace. Far too often, women descend the corporate ladder due to harassment based on their fear. Showing your femininity (within reason) in the workplace is acceptable and should not be taken as an invitation for inexcusable behavior. Antonia stood up for herself and we could all take a page out of Antonia's book in regard to her courageous and decisive traits. No one will advocate for you the way you will. Use your voice.

When I was younger, I was told to be "nice." Being female is not about being nice. Being a female is about being respected and respectable. Not everyone is going to like you. Not everyone is going to be your friend. Spoiler alert! You are not going to like everyone you come across, and that is okay, so long as you treat others with respect. If you show respect, you will attract respect in return. When in doubt, channel the golden rule: do unto others as you would have them do unto you.

GAYLE'S PRESCRIPTION TO BE COURAGEOUS & STAND UP FOR YOURSELF

1. Always stand up for yourself. Speak up, communicate with respect and dignity. Report / document issue(s) in the workplace by sending an email as well as meeting with Human Resources.

2. Conquer your fears of personal and professional reinvention with courage.

3. Identify your unique superpowers. Those are your strengths that no one can take away from you. Your superpowers set you apart from your competition.

4. Take the Codebreakers Technologies B.A.N.K.® personality profile assessment tool to understand your superpowers (and the superpowers of others) for stronger and more productive conversations. This is an excellent activity for teams to take to achieve better productivity and more beneficial business outcomes, as well as for candidates for hire to assess their strengths and whether or not they would compliment a team and/or an organization's dynamics. Crack your code using the Codebreakers Personality Coding Technology assessment tool to understand your superpowers: https://www.mybankcode.com/TheodoraSpeaks

   Codebreaker Technology: B.A.N.K.® is the world's only sales methodology scientifically validated to accurately predict buying behavior in real time.

It's also a tool to utilize when seeking to understand the person / people / audience you are trying to reach. My clients take the assessment test to identify their superpowers and to learn how to communicate with people on their team with a different code. Another way I use Codebreaker Technologies is when I am researching someone on LinkedIn to better understand who they are and how they communicate so that I can be relatable and authentic when building a relationship with them.

5. Identify a list of strategies you could use to communicate with other types of individuals both similar and different from you.

My "aha" moment was when I was pregnant with my second daughter. I spoke on the big stage before 10,000 Microsoft attendees and discovered my voice, learning how my words impacted thousands. Both virtually and in-person, I offer keynotes, presentations, workshops, and breakouts to revitalize and empower gender inclusivity efforts at large and mid-sized organizations and universities. Speaking to an audience fills my heart, and I feel called to motivate and influence others to take their leaps of faith. I enjoy inspiring others to shine.

CAREER RESOURCES FROM GAYLE

Presentation skills are such an important tool to have in your toolbox. Presence commands attention. If you are able to cultivate strong public speaking skills, you will earn the respect of others because you can command an audience's attention. Mastering the art of public speaking is the #1 trait to develop to boost your career. Warren Buffett says it best: "Now, you can improve your value by 50 percent just by learning communication skills—public speaking."

In addition to my professional coaching and consulting work, I offer public speaking training to level-up presentation skills and presence and how to apply them to one's personal brand.

PILLAR 5: BALANCE

MAALIKA, THE BALANCED MATHEMATICIAN

The ghost, clown, and witch scampered by, nearly knocking Maalika over as they raced next door to collect their Halloween candy.

"Sheesh!" Maalika exclaimed. She heard the house's door open simultaneously with the little rascals' exuberant shouts of "Trick-or-treat!"

Her friend Geeta laughed. "We are going to be killed by miniature monsters on the hunt to increase their candy stash."

"And all we want to do is cross the street to get to Amanda's party," Maalika shouted as more trick-or-treaters ran past them on the crosswalk.

"Do you know what I did when I was younger, Geeta?"

"Noooo. Do I *want* to know?" Geeta jabbed Maalika in the ribs.

"I loved math so much as a kid. Still do, obviously. After mom and dad inspected the candy, I used to sort each of them by name, in alphabetical order. Then, I added the names and amounts to a spreadsheet and created a bar chart!" Maalika laughed. "I was such an organized, chart-loving girl."

"You still are!" Geeta exclaimed.

"So true. So true." Maalika agreed.

Her phone rang with a face-time from her boss, Trayvon. He looked frazzled. His face looked very strained, and his geo afro was completely disheveled, like he had been in a fight during a thunderstorm.

"Trayvon! What's going on? Do you have your costume? Are you coming to Amanda's party? What are the kids' costumes?"

"Maalika," he said, his voice uncharacteristically stern. "I'm not wasting my time on Halloween. It's a made-up holiday, and I have no use for its foolishness!"

Maalika stepped back and away from her friends.

"Tray," she stammered.

"Don't 'Tray' me, Maalika. You think we're friends? We work together. I'm your boss. I can't believe you aren't in the office, fixing the reports you screwed up."

"Reports? Screwed up? What are you seeing?" Maalika asked.

"What am I seeing? Clearly what you are not seeing!" he started raising his voice. "That's okay. Don't you worry about it, Princess. The rest of the world will wait for you to get done with your party."

He rolled his eyes and hung up the phone. Maalika sat down, stunned.

"What was that?" Geeta asked worriedly. Maalika had stepped aside to take the call and not disturb Geeta in case she wanted to get to Amanda's. Geeta could tell by the look on Maalika's face that something was wrong.

"That was the worst and strangest call I've ever received from Trayvon. I'm not sure what that was, and I know I didn't deserve it no matter what I screwed up. He's off the rails tonight. I'll have to figure it out later. I can't let his stuff ruin my fun night with you, Amanda, and our friends."

"A candy bar chart, Maalika? I don't know if that's genius or too meticulous," Geeta returned to the conversation before the call, hoping it would take the edge off Maalika so she could focus on some fun—which she deserved.

"Haha. Probably a little bit of both. It motivated me to hit more houses, that's for sure. I have records from fifth through eighth grade on Excel. My mom has pictures of younger years of my candy sorted.

"Did you know that, at least in my parents' neighborhood, the best year for trick-or-treating was 2017? I noticed it when I went with my brother and sister's kids. They had boatloads. I think they gathered more than I ever did. Then, in 2018 and 2019, there were less houses participating. In 2020, with the pandemic, it was shut down, and in 2021, even fewer households participated than 2019. I'm wondering if it's a dying tradition, especially with the more health-conscious generations," Maalika explained as they approached the front door of their colleague Amanda's house.

"That's interesting, Maalika. I've never thought that much about the 'Trends of Trick-or-Treating.' You could be on to something. That actually could be a book title." Geeta laughed.

"Finally! You're here!" Amanda exclaimed as she swung open the door. "It's about time. I can't play my favorite Bollywood music until my girlfriend is here. C'mon in!"

Maalika and Amanda kissed hello, and Geeta fiercely hugged Amanda, which was equally matched. The three worked together at a large consumer packaged goods company in the finance department. All were math whizzes, but Maalika led large teams across business units, as she was a true mathematical genius. She clearly demonstrated her love of math whenever they were poised with a pricing issue. Her talent was that she was able to look at it from a telescopic view just as easily as she could view it through a microscopic lens—she was both a "big picture" *and* "detail-oriented" person.

Geeta and Amanda led the internal teams in two separate business units. They had become close friends from early on in their careers, starting with having lunch together in the company cafeteria. Over the years, they cheered each other's successes and supported each other through the challenges they faced. It's not always easy to navigate a three-person friendship, but they were committed to open communication, honesty, and empowering each other, rather than competing against each other.

The party was already in full swing as they walked through the foyer and hall to the backyard, where the dance floor DJ played music and the guests danced. Halloween happened to be the same day as Amanda's birthday, and she threw a huge bash every year to celebrate. They were so close to one another that Amanda invited Maalika's and Geeta's parents, siblings, nieces, and nephews. They bobbed for apples, they trick or treated around the neighborhood, and played Halloween-themed games. Maalika led the competition for the most stable and most interesting Lego structure. As a young girl, she spent countless hours with her Lego collection. Even as an adult, when she was stressed, she pulled out her Legos and assembled some type of creature, building, village, or garden.

Amanda was the "hostess with the mostess" who loved to include everyone she knew, make everyone feel comfortable, and celebrate life with all those she loved. She had built the life she loved and wanted to share her gifts on her birthday. Every year, each invitation requested the "presence" of her guests, and if they would like to contribute a "present," they should consider making a donation to whichever nonprofit she selected that year. This year, she suggested three organizations for the guests to consider for their donations. She picked United Way, her parents' favorite nonprofit that they supported, her own favorite organization, UNICEF, which she had been supporting since she was fifteen years old, and, to show Maalika how much she meant to her, Amanda included the organization where they both volunteered, Feeding America.

In typical fashion, Maalika found her own parents in the kitchen, serving food and making sure everything ran smoothly. Since she was a little girl, her family loved cooking together. It was in the kitchen that she started to understand math in measurements, which led to her love of planning, preparing, and cooking the meals. Beyond that, her mom always said, "Love is in the details," and insisted that all of the kids learn how to set a proper table. Napkin folded in half to the left of the plate, the fork on top of the napkin, the knife and spoon on the right with the glass above them. She could set a beautiful table in her sleep, and at friends' houses, she always found herself "fixing" the place settings out of habit. Even today, she can't help herself when it comes to dressing a table. When she started dating Amanda, they had fun quarreling about the proper location for the fork, and Amanda purposefully misplaced all the table setting pieces upside down and side by side just to rile Maalika.

At Maalika's house, dinner always led with a prayer of gratitude, followed by good manners and wonderful table conversations. Her mom and dad were both good cooks and counted on the children to contribute to the meal. Since each of them could walk, they were taught how to mix curry in with the chicken, cut carrots for the salad, and count everything twice—the pinches of salt, the teaspoons, tablespoons, and other measurements. There was always some type of soup in the freezer as a backup plan for those nights where a new experimental meal didn't work out.

In the time her family spent together, the deep connections they forged with each other, and the engaging conversation at dinnertime, Maalika learned the value of planning out her time, balancing family, play, self-care, and work. After school, her parents required they have at least an hour of play to break free from the rigid school schedule, then homework, dinner, reading time, and resting time before bed. Schedules, structure, and consistency were key to success for a family of seven.

Oh, and patience. Her parents were the most patient people on the planet. It was fitting for the order, calmness, and intention they operated with as a couple, and as parents who modeled an intricately woven balance in every aspect of life. Often, people mentioned how Maalika brought calmness and peace to her friends and family. While some houses she visited were filled with chaos and the parents and siblings lacked patience, Maalika was born into it. She often wondered, *Why can't everyone be Zen like Buddha?*

In the kitchen, Maalika helped her mom assemble some dishes and remove those that needed to be refilled. Hearing the first two beats of her favorite song by Arijit Singh, she whipped her head up, kissed her mom briefly, and ran to the dance floor, doing her most prominent Bollywood dance moves. It was a party to remember. Taking the time to celebrate family, friends, and the birthday of the woman who just may become her future life partner was a prime example of Maalika's balance between work, life, self-care, and play.

It was a brisk November morning. Maalika shuddered as she pulled her green and gold headscarf around her dark brown hair, which was pulled back in a neat and tidy bun.

"These headscarves are not made for warmth," she muttered under her breath. "I should have brought my heavier wrap. Why do I always forget how cold the bite of the wind becomes this time of year?"

Arriving at her office, she hung up her coat, unpacked her laptop, and headed straight for the breakroom.

"Aiyo!" Maalika said, rubbing her hands together.

"Aiyo is right! Cold enough for you, Maalika?" mimicked Trayvon as he walked up to the coffee machine.

"Hey, Tray! How was your weekend?" Maalika wanted to start the day lighthearted, considering the phone call on Halloween. She didn't want to cause any waves. So far so good.

"Alright. Yours?"

"Good. We missed you at Amanda's party. I think that's the first time you've ever missed in eleven years."

"Stop overreacting. It hasn't been eleven years. Halloween is way too much work for me," Trayvon replied as he added cream to his coffee.

Maalika was taken aback. *"Stop overreacting;"* he'd never spoken to her like that. Stranger still, Halloween had always been a favorite holiday of his. His whole family had dressed up as Disney movie characters every year for the past eleven years, and he usually spearheaded it.

Another couple of tick marks to keep track of and a little burn inside that I'll have to cool down from later. Just like the comments from that awful weekend phone call, Maalika thought to herself and filed away in her brain.

"What do we have on the schedule today, Maalika?"

"Well, Boss, we have this electrifying team meeting at ten with the execs, and then you and I are running through the shoe packaging for Elite's summer collection." Maalika tried to muster up some enthusiasm, but the sting was burning.

"Electrifying? Hmmm. Why don't we take our Elite meeting off-site for lunch? I need to get out of here."

"Sure. I'll make reservations. Usual?"

"Yeah, that'll work. Thanks, Lika," he murmured over his shoulder as he headed for his office.

Maalika finished stirring her coffee, grabbed an apple, and needed to vent, or her whole day would be off-kilter. She popped into one of the private conference rooms and called Amanda. Tears came to her eyes as she replayed the two off-putting and insulting comments from Trayvon. She couldn't understand what was happening. As usual, Amanda listened intently, encouraging her to take a couple of deep breaths and to try to put it behind her so she could get through her day. Trayvon had said a couple of off comments over the years that rubbed her the wrong way. Maybe he was having a bad few days.

"Thanks, Amanda. Love you," Maalika hung up the phone, dodged into the bathroom to wipe her eyes, freshen her eye makeup, and touch up her lipstick. She fluffed her hair, took a couple of deep breaths, stood in her Wonder Woman power pose for one minute, and headed back to her office feeling much better.

As she approached her desk in the open area right outside Trayvon's office, she noticed something strange. The hallway was darker than usual.

"Hmm. Tray closed his window blinds. He loves the sun. Even though it's windy and damp out, the sunshine is usually something Trayvon enjoys seeing through the windows." Maalika said to herself.

Crash! Bam!

"Damn it!"

Maalika jumped out of her chair and ran out of her office to the hall to find out more about the commotion—and, more importantly, where it was coming from.

Bam. Bam. Bam.

Maalika's head spun towards Trayvon's office.

"Oh my gosh!" she exclaimed, bolting towards the door.

"Trayvon! What is happening?" she whisper-shouted as she swung the door open. Co-workers were starting to stick their heads out of their offices. She quietly shut the door behind her. Trayvon was pacing and had a glass vase in his hand.

"Let's put the vase down, Tray," Maalika spoke kindly and gently to him.

"Maalika, what the hell?" Trayvon shouted. " I overheard your phone call with your girlfriend, Amanda, and it pissed me off. What is wrong with you? Stop exaggerating. Can I express *any* negative feelings around you without you getting paranoid about it?"

Maalika took a few steps back and moved towards the door, frightened for the first time ever in all the years she had worked with Trayvon. He continued, "You know, Maalika, you aren't perfect either!"

"Whoa, Trayvon," Maalika said in a semi-stern voice. It felt like there was a peach pit stuck in her throat. She cleared her throat, swallowed, and, in a steady voice, said, "Trayvon, you are not going to talk with me this way. Whatever is going on, you will get through it, but I am not going to be your scapegoat here. I'll be back in an hour. If you are calm, we can talk. This is not okay."

As Maalika turned and walked out the door, Trayvon watched her, puzzled. He looked at the vase, then the mess around his office, and then her. He shook his head, carefully placing the tall blue vase on his credenza. He walked to his couch, sat down, and buried his face in his hands.

Maalika started working for her current employer eleven years ago. Trayvon took a liking to her after observing her work ethic, her analytical skills, and her empowering approach to working with others. She hadn't been in a leadership role at the time, yet her co-workers, naturally and without words, nominated her as their group's leader. In a short time, Maalika had become well-liked and well-respected by the executive team. When it came time for him to pick a candidate to mentor and sponsor, she was his first choice.

With her great reputation, he found it surprising that he had been granted his top preference.

From the moment Maalika shook Trayvon's hand eleven years ago, she knew he was a special man. He was kind, interested, and sharp as a tack. She was pleased he was to become her professional, in-house mentor. She loved her job and couldn't imagine working anywhere else. From the early days, Trayvon had almost treated her like a sister and figuratively held her hand along the way through her career, guiding her through company politics and towards the goals she wanted to achieve. Every time she was promoted, he sat down with her to help her think about the next two roles she wanted to reach and design the roadmap for how she could achieve those goals. He encouraged her to find a mentor outside of the company, a sponsor inside the company to rally for her in the boardroom, and a business coach independent of the company. He explained that his networks inside and outside of the company were the key groups of people who continuously offered him support, encouragement, and sounding boards.

Unlike the majority of professionals who do not take the advice from their mentors, Maalika hung on every word and took advantage of every opportunity. She felt fortunate for having a position she loved that offered significant benefits. She loved money and commissions and thought her earnings were fabulous. Additionally, the equity shares, 401K, and bonuses prepared her for the future quite well. She agreed with the company's mission to minimize its carbon footprint, so she reinvested her savings and stocks directly into the company. Lika was good with numbers, especially when it came to balancing earnings, expenses, savings, and investments.

Her dad taught her and her siblings how to save and invest in the stock market. Every Sunday, they read the paper, reviewed the stock section, and launched into their weekly family game where they chose a stock, invested in it, and watched it on the NASDAQ. With seven kids, everything became a competition. Buy low, sell high, or trade. She even had designed a spin-off of the game with pretend coins to teach her younger siblings how it was done. They tracked which stocks did well and which did not. It was fun—and beneficial, as, over the years, it afforded her the ability to collect a respectable sum, from which she drew to hire her external business coach and splurge on an upgrade to her kitchen. In fact, her friends and colleagues were so intrigued with her interest and winnings in stocks that she launched a women's investment club within the company because, historically, young men were taught to save their money and women were not. It was fun to see the women win investments, pay off their debt, remodel various parts of their houses, and go on unexpected vacations.

Hands down, Trayvon was a major contributor to her success. As a result, their relationship had become stronger and changed over the years. From being his mentee, Maalika went on to join one of Tray's teams for a few projects, and now, they worked on the same team while Trayvon supervised. The supervisory role met formal requirements, but the two saw each other as equals and close friends; neither dared to cross professional boundaries when it came to their "official roles." Until today.

"Amanda, I'm so sorry to bother you again," Maalika interjected Amanda's greeting over the phone. She needed some sound advice and support. "You won't believe what just happened!"

Maalika described the events of the morning.

"Lika, I'm so sorry. That's horrible, and I'm so glad you stood up for yourself with professionalism and courage," Amanda sympathized.

"I thought I was going to die. I've never had to do that to a boss before. I normally would have just started cleaning up the broken glass and let whatever he said to me be swept under the rug."

"Well, you did it, and now you are here. Take a breath," Amanda advised. "So, what do you think is going on?"

"For the last few months, he has not been himself. I never thought he would blow up at me, though, and I didn't want to pry."

"Well, for starters, this wasn't just a 'blow-up.' This sounds like a poster board example of employee gaslighting," Amanda explained.

"What is gaslighting?" Maalika asked, puzzled.

"It's the same crap I dealt with from my ex. They have something going on, and try to blame you, make you the scapegoat, undermine you so they feel better about themselves, and even make you feel like you are the cause of all of it."

"This feels exactly like that. And it's icky."

"It is totally icky," Amanda agreed. "It took me months of therapy to understand it, recognize it, and realize that it was her and not me. Has Tray been doing this to you a lot?"

"No, I would say this was the first time he's been belligerent, insulting, and accusatory. He's said off or weird comments before, but nothing like this. What should I do?"

"What do you think you should do? How did you leave it?"

"I told him I would be back in an hour, and if he was calm, we could talk," Maalika recalled.

"Okay. That was a good forewarning. It gives you the upper hand and sets your boundaries," Amanda encouraged.

"I'm feeling like he and I should have a long conversation over lunch. I should bring up the past few months and see if I can mention that I think he may be depressed."

"Oh, boy. You would know. That's not going to be easy. Members of the Black community generally have an aversion to talking about depression. They are strong people."

"I'll approach it very lightly. I should know how to do this. I've had it, gone through therapy, and then helped some family members recognize it in themselves, so I think I can handle it. It's a little daunting that I have to do it with my boss."

"You can handle it, Maalika! Do you remember what you were like when you were depressed, and your therapist helped you recognize it so you could live a more balanced life with more fun in it?"

"That's right! At my breaking point, I acted just like Tray. Wow. I really feel more empathy for him now than anger. I get it. Okay, I'll definitely have a heart-to-heart with him about this today. I want him to take some positive steps forward so he can feel and live better."

"You are so amazing, Maalika! You've got this!" Amanda cheered.

"Thanks, for helping me figure it out, Amanda."

Maalika hung up the phone, headed outside for a walk. She needed some fresh air to clean up the emotional cobwebs. A quick two mile walk would put her in a better headspace and heart space. As she thought of the past eleven years, she recalled mostly good times, but the last few months had been rough. And now, she realized just how much Tray had been struggling. Maalika's heart went out to him, as she had been concerned for a while. Maalika rapped on the partially open door to Trayvon's office.

"Come in," Trayvon said quietly from the couch. He sounded exhausted, defeated, unsure, embarrassed, and humiliated, all at once.

Maalika walked over and sat next to him.

"Lika, this is too much. I don't know what is happening to me."

"I'm sorry, Tray. I've noticed it's been a rough few months for you. Let's go to lunch. We'll be a little early, but that's okay. I reserved the private table," Maalika said as she stood up, headed to her office to pick up her coat.

It was a ten-minute walk to their favorite Indian cuisine restaurant, and Maalika had to get her thoughts in order before they got there. The time for the talk she anticipated having for a while had finally arrived.

Trayvon and Maalika walked quickly through the cold drizzle coming down on that November day. When they arrived at the restaurant and stepped inside, the warmth of its interior hit them at the same time as the aroma from the kitchen. It was nice to be somewhere familiar amid the stress of the day. After taking off their coats and hanging them on the hook outside their private booth, they slid into their seats across from each other.

"Tea?"

"Yes, please." They both said in unison.

"Green tea with ginger, please," Maalika requested.

They sat there in silence for a few minutes and turned off their phones. When the server came with the tea, they grabbed the warm cups with both hands, inhaled, and took a sip to warm their bones.

Maalika looked at Tray and understood she was going to have to lead this conversation. She took a quiet, deep breath, summoned her inner courage to keep her emotions out of this conversation and to be able to guide him appropriately to open up, hear her concerns, and consider her suggestions.

"Tray, I'm worried about you," she quietly said with empathy in her eyes.

He looked at her with a brief flinch of eye contact.

"You know me. I'm not going to judge anything. I'm here to support you in any way I can," she continued.

"I know," he responded, his tone a blend of gruffness and understanding. "I'm really sorry that I stepped out of line and said such mean things to you. I don't know what came over me this morning. I really regret it."

"Share with me, please. How are you feeling these days?" Maalika inquired.

"Lika, I'm not sure. I'm kinda disorganized, can't focus, lack motivation, and I'm angry a lot. You don't see a portion of it. I stuff it all down, so it doesn't come out, which just makes me angrier."

"I can see you are hurting and struggling. It hasn't been an easy few months for you. I've been worried for a while. I've noticed some of these changes and just thought you were having a bad day, but then, I saw the same actions and behaviors happen again over the following weeks."

"Really? I'm sorry to bother you."

"It's no bother! We are close friends. Tray, I'm here for you anytime you need me."

"That's the thing, Lika, I don't know that I need anything. I don't know what is happening to me."

"Tray, as friends, we care about each other. We can read each other well, almost better than our partners can read us. I've been wondering if you might have depression."

"Depression? How do you figure that?" He asked, a little confused.

"Well, there is a lot that most of us don't know about mental health challenges, and we express symptoms differently from each other."

"I'm not laying in bed all day, Lika. I'm here today, aren't I?" He rebutted. It stung Maalika a bit.

"It's not that stereotypical. Significant changes in the way we normally behave can become clues to what our own depression looks like."

Trayvon watched her, looking inquisitive. She felt comfortable to continue.

"I've noticed over the past few months that you are late to work every day, and you are not going to the gym before work. Your temper is short, which I've never seen before in our eleven years working together—leading to incidents just like what happened in the office today."

"Really? How long have you noticed this?" Trayvon asked with a surprised expression.

"About three to four months. It was sporadic for the first couple, but in the last four weeks or so, I've seen it happen more frequently."

"I had no idea. I am feeling like the weight of the world is on my shoulders, and that everything is moving so quickly. I don't have time for work, for family, and I've even stopped working out or caring about my health. I feel like I'm ready to give it all up because I can't get… like… balanced or something. I feel like everything is out of whack."

"That's how it can happen for some of us. And that's *okay*. It's so important to maintain balance in our lives. I went to therapy for a long time to get that balance and figure it out. It's not easy. Have you talked to Jazz about how you are feeling?"

"Not really. We've been arguing more frequently than usual. I think we want to bite each other's heads off. She keeps asking me, 'What's wrong, Tray?' I have no idea, so how am I going to answer her?"

"Well, maybe now that we've talked, you can work with her to help you make some sense of it. There are lots of options out there to help you, and you can find the right steps for treatment with your doctor. It's been a while, and the experts say that if you are struggling for two weeks or more, you need to talk to a medical doctor as soon as possible."

"What are they going to do?"

"They'll ask a bunch of questions to assess your current lifestyle and mental state, and, if there's a diagnosis, they'll discuss which treatment they recommend," Maalika explained.

"Okay. I can do that."

"I also want to give you some numbers to keep on your speed dial. One of the things your doctor may recommend is a therapist. The website Psychology Today has lists of therapists in your local area. Check them out. Also, this book, *Burnout: The Secret to Unlocking the Stress Cycle* by Emily Nagoski, PhD and Amelia Nagoski, DMA is awesome. It helped me. I'll send the Audible version to you."

"Thanks. That does sound good," Trayvon agreed as he looked through the sample pages on his phone.

Maalika approached the next question cautiously, praying that the answer was no. "Have you had any dark thoughts about not living any longer?"

"No. I love Jazz and our kids too much. I would never want to leave them. But I have wondered. I just wouldn't go through with it."

"Oh, Tray. I'm sorry you've been dealing with those feelings alone. I'm so glad you trust me enough to say so. I'm going to give you the numbers to the Suicide Prevention Lifeline, too—only because if you should start thinking darker thoughts, you'll have the number in your speed dial. You can also call them even if it's just a flash in your mind to talk to them about how you can stop thinking about it."

"Okay. So the first thing I should do is see my doctor, and then check out Psychology Today?" Trayvon asked.

"Yes," Maalika responded, surprised and pleased that he was so receptive to getting help.

"Will you go to the doctor as soon as possible and talk to your wife about how you are feeling?"

"Yes!"

"That's terrific, Tray. I'm so proud of you. How are you feeling?"

"Surprisingly, Lika," he chuckled, "This is the best I've felt in a long time. I had no idea it could be depression. I just thought I was turning into a middle-aged, grumpy old man!"

"Well, let's get you back to your happy-go-lucky, charming, middle-aged self!"

"Deal!" Trayvon laughed out loud. It was the first genuine smile she'd seen him make in a long time.

Whew, Maalika thought to herself. *That went so much better than I could have imagined.*

As they ordered their lunch, the air around them felt lighter. They began discussing the Elite project.

The two put on their coats and quickly returned to their offices. The cleaning crew had been summoned to clean up and repair Trayvon's broken items, and no one was to be seen within eyesight. A little embarrassed, he breathed a huge sigh of relief, grateful for the grace and forgiveness extended by his colleagues.

Maalika paced slowly back and forth along the windows in the conference room, watching the pedestrians quickly dodge in and out of cars and buildings to avoid the rain and cold. She reflected on her day and was grateful for the gift of having a productive and hopeful conversation with her close confidante. She was shaken by the experience. It hit so close to home, both because she cared about him so deeply and because, to some extent, she knew what he was going through. It was to be expected. The weight of the world felt heavy on her shoulders, as she became concerned for all of those that were suffering with depression. However, she had no doubt this conversation would lead to a positive outcome for Trayvon and his family.

"Ahhh. Life would be just a wee bit easier," she said to herself quietly, "if only everyone could be Zen like Buddha."

MAALIKA'S REFLECTION & PLAN TO ACHIEVE BALANCED WELLNESS

Maalika's wish is to get us talking about mental health challenges so we can understand how to better help others and ourselves. With her therapist, her main work was to find "Balance" in her life, and it has become her superpower. At one point in her life, she worked more than anything else and realized she had become depressed and anxious. After getting treatment and seeing a therapist, she was able to get back on track and feel more like herself. It's a concerted effort every day to keep balance and harmony in her life, and she has seen the benefits. Through her experience with depression and anxiety, she learned a lot about the symptoms and how to help others through it. She was able to help family members, and, when Trayvon showed signs, she knew how to handle it, even though she was nervous about it.

Once she saw the need to engage, she took steps to figure out how she would approach the situation and how she would offer ideas for him to consider. Follow along with Maalika as she shares her decision-making process with you.

STEP 1 – AWARENESS

Once she recognized Trayvon needed some friendly guidance, she considered the situation and how addressing it could result in a positive outcome.

What was the situation?

Trayvon is normally jovial, hardworking, and focused. Over the past four months, Maalika noticed slight changes in Trayvon's behaviors throughout the day and his responses to various situations. At first, she shrugged them off because we all have bad days, but then, the frequency increased. He seemed to have lost his focus, his humor, and his happy-go-lucky personality. Instead, he seemed stressed, he was coming to work late, and he wasn't meeting deadlines. He was angry, not so nurturing, and seemed so sad. He was more secretive and defensive about his activities, like he had been on Halloween, and had made it a practice to stay in his office for lunch. None of these were his normal behaviors.

With her heightened empathy towards people who are struggling, she knew it was time to talk with him privately.

How was it affecting others?

Family. Typically, if behavior changes at work, it certainly changes at home. This conversation could put him on notice to get the help he needs to smooth out any issues or poor behavior at home.

Work. The team was not hitting the numbers and a couple of big projects were delayed. The customers had submitted change orders on the design, so it wasn't the fault of the teams. However, they were used to exceeding the numbers and being over their goals in all areas.

The teams lived for their bonuses and commissions, which were never limited by a glass ceiling. Times had been different since the pandemic. Customers and employers were more conservative, which led to a reduction in quarterly and annual revenue goals. It impacted everyone's income goals. Unlike other companies, the decreases hit everyone from the executives down. It was a shared loss or success for each employee.

Clearly, Trayvon was feeling the stress, and understandably so. However, slamming his door and breaking his decor was unacceptable at work—or anywhere. Since it reached that level, he needed this conversation as the first step.

Health. Trayvon had been more tired than ever before. He had stopped seeing his trainer, stopped going to the gym altogether, and seemed to be eating a lot of fast food, which was very unusual for him. Maalika could tell he had gained a bit of weight. Those are the symptoms Maalika noticed at work. There are several other symptoms he may have that she couldn't see. She understood. Whenever her life was out of balance, health was the first thing that went out the window.

STEP 2 – OPTIONS

What were her options?

After her walk, Maalika had two options.

1. Return to work and sweep the entire experience under the rug.

2. Talk to Trayvon and mention having a conversation about his problems.

STEP 3 – RISK v. REWARD

If Maalika did approach him, what would she risk? What would be the greater reward?

If she chose to take action, what risks might she encounter? Are they worth it?

Some people are not receptive to hearing they might have depression or anxiety. There is difficulty in going against cultural norms, as well as gender norms, to have an honest and productive conversation about mental health that will lead to positive outcomes. If Trayvon did not respond well to talking about depression, it could be a very uncomfortable conversation if not handled properly, and might even make him more resistant to being open with others or getting the help he needs. Additionally, it could put a cloud over their relationship.

If she chose to take action, what would be the benefits? Are they worth it?

With her heightened empathy towards people who are struggling, she knew it was time to talk with him privately. As his closest female colleague, Maalika was probably the only one willing to have the conversation with him. She knew what to look for in terms of symptoms of mental health challenges, as several of her relatives suffered from depression and anxiety. Her parents were very open about family health issues so Maalika and her siblings could recognize it and ask for help.

Trayvon is Maalika's closest friend and best boss. Their trust for each other filtered into all aspects of their life. They were each other's confidante. If she can't have this conversation with him, his wife would be the only other person. However, mental health issues are tricky, and when living with someone, it's hard to dissect and recognize the symptoms in them as the changes slowly creep into everyday life.

The benefits far outweighed the risk because, by having that conversation, Trayvon could get the help he needed to get back on track and feel more like himself. Once he was there, his relationship with his family and friends and his work life would drastically improve.

STEP 4 – APPROACH

What was the best approach?

Maalika felt that, since they had worked together for eleven years and considered each other family, she would slowly approach Trayvon with some light questions to get him to start talking. She knew she had to make sure she did not come across as judgmental, because that would cause him to close up. Specific questions would be most helpful to offer him some options for support. It's a careful line to walk, because no one wants to make the other person feel uncomfortable, insecure, or judged about possible mental health challenges like depression and anxiety.

STEP 5 – AGENT FOR CHANGE

Find Courage. Like every conversation with her family members she helped, she had to muster up a lot of courage to have this conversation with the man who, ultimately, is her boss first. She thought lunch at a public place would be a comfortable environment.

Tone. Maalika knew her first words would set the tone and pace. She would either turn him away or open him to talk. She wanted it to be a conversation, not a lecture.

Desired Outcome. Above everything else, Maalika wanted to support him in any way he needed and be available when he wanted to talk, vent, or anything else. Additionally, Maalika wanted to make sure he wasn't having thoughts of ending his life by suicide.

Resources. Sometimes, when a difficult conversation happens, it's never talked about again. Since this could be the only chance she had to talk, she wanted to make sure she encouraged him to talk with his wife, schedule an appointment with his doctor, find a therapist, and give him resources for therapists and lifelines. She knew to have a list of local therapists, the psychologytoday.com website, and the lifelines for mental health and suicide prevention on hand.

GAYLE'S REFLECTIONS ON BALANCE & MENTAL HEALTH

Mental health issues have significantly increased since the pandemic began in 2020. It takes all of us to look out for each other and recognize significant unusual changes in behaviors and actions in ourselves and others. If you or someone you know has changed significantly and has behaved negatively for two weeks or longer, it's time to seek medical attention. Otherwise, it can get worse. A full list of symptoms of depression and anxiety can be found at NAMI.org, WebMD.com, or MayoClinic.com. There is no shame or stigma in taking care of ourselves. Developing strategies to cope with mental illness is just like caring for diabetes, high blood pressure, high cholesterol, or any other medical disease. Our health and well-being is the most important thing to our own selves and those who love us.

GAYLE'S PRESCRIPTION TO PROMOTE BALANCED WELLNESS AT HOME & AT WORK

1. If you or someone you know struggles with mental wellness and well-being, talk to them and recommend the organizations Maalika listed.

2. Balance is not a 50/50 scale. In the world we live in, thanks to the global pandemic, the lines have become blurred between work and home. The perception of a "balanced" life has been replaced with work / life integration, requiring a laser focused approach to our priorities. Picture two interlocking circles. We need to learn how to optimize our efforts within the gray matter between the two circles.

3. Through loss, troubleshooting, pivoting, and failure we learn the most about ourselves, so share stories of failure and loss with others to help lessen their struggle.

4. What does not permanently tarnish us makes us stronger and more resilient, so step into your power.

5. Burnout is real. Stress and stressors will happen in life and come from places such as work, home, family, or your community. If you ignore the stressors, you cannot address the root causes to find a clear mind and open heart. When you address your stressors head-on, you approach life from a place of balance, authenticity, passion, and grace.

Throughout my entire career, I have greatly benefited from relying on my mentors, sponsors, therapists, and now, business coaches. I believe and invest in them, and they have empowered me to take my leaps of faith, and, one day, I had the confidence to jump off the diving board, into the unknown. Through their encouragement, I designed my career blueprint to incorporate all of my dreams. They held me accountable at every turn throughout my reinvention journey; they were sounding boards for my ideas. Hiring a business coach can seem like an investment. It is, and you get what you pay for. You are making an investment in yourself and your future because they are in the trenches with you, helping shape your future with you. When you find the right fit for you, they save you from making the same mistakes they did, they prevent you from having to learn the hard lessons, and they save you tens of thousands of dollars. They are in your trusted circle.

RESOURCES FROM GAYLE

FOR YOUR CAREER

If you find yourself wanting to explore how your life, business, and career could look when you partner with a coach, reach out to me at https://www.gaylekeller.org. I offer individual 1:1 career coaching to set goals and guide you to achieve them. My group coaching programs are themed based on various lessons I've covered here in the book and others. I have one program that incorporates the lessons learned from each of these characters in this book.

FOR MENTAL HEALTH

If you or someone you know struggles with mental health challenges like depression, anxiety, dark thoughts and/or is contemplating ending their life by suicide, please reach out to any of these numbers today to speak with a trained counselor who will help you with support, help your friend with support, or answer any questions you may have.

I encourage you to always have these numbers in your speed dial, for you or for a friend. You never know when you may need them, and sometimes, we don't know where to turn when help is needed. When you call, you will get the support you need and deserve so you can live a life with fewer struggles. There is a counselor waiting every day, every hour, throughout the year to talk with you or your friend.

Suicide Prevention Lifelines

US National Suicide Lifeline 24/365
SuicidePreventionLifeline.org
1-800-273-8255 / 911
In English, Spanish & For Deaf & Hard of Hearing

International Suicide Prevention Lifelines
https://www.opencounseling.com/suicide-hotlines

Mental Health Lifelines

Substance Abuse & Mental Health Services Administration 24/365
SAMHSA.gov
1-800-622-4357

PsychologyToday.com/US
Find a therapist in your area

Employer/Employee Programs

EAP - Employee Assistance Programs
Benefits Department - List of In-Network Therapists

EPILOGUE

The first rays of sunlight played peek-a-boo among the trees. Birdsong filled the retreat center with nature's music, and the air was filled with the tantalizing aroma of an early breakfast that wafted from the kitchen. On the second day of the retreat program, the ladies started joining Silla on the back deck for coffee to reflect on the day before. It was so peaceful.

"Has anyone seen Theodora? I'm looking forward to our second day. I started reading her book last night and ordered her children's book series for my nieces," Antonia said.

"Not yet. I think the facilitators stay in the guest house down the road," shared Tyriqa.

"Mmmm. Good morning, ladies! Breakfast smells delicious. I thought I would never need to eat after yesterday's meals. Our chef is spoiling us. I'm shocked how hungry I am today." Elaine said.

"Well, self-love and self-confidence are major workouts!" Antonia laughed.

All thc ladies laughed along with her. The day before ended successfully as the small groups bonded together during the interactive activities and private journaling time. It was a special retreat for women in S.T.E.A.M. to break free from the daily rigor of life, family, and careers so they could reflect, reset, and ready themselves for the year ahead and set longer term goals for themselves. Several groups stayed up late, sharing stories and dreams with each other. The real bonding happened in late night talks or at the bar. And it was always about something interesting. Both Tyriqa and Antoina shared a love for Wonder Woman!

Tyriqa looked around at the group of ladies who had become her friends and was relieved that the environment was the complete opposite of her usual dealings with colleagues. After 20 years in Tech, she had found a group of women who shared the same values as her and preferred to empower other women rather than compete against them. She had great hope for the day ahead and drank her coffee as she pushed back and forth in her rocker.

Just then, the dinner bell rang, signaling the ladies to the dining room for breakfast.

"And now, ladies, it's time for our next breakout room," Theodora, the retreat facilitator and organizer, introduced the next part of the retreat. "We covered 'Courage,' 'Confidence,' 'Decisiveness,' and 'Assertiveness' over the last two days. Our next and last breakout session will be on 'Balance and Goal Setting.' Please grab your journals, writing instruments, and water on your way to your assigned rooms. Your facilitator will lead the discussion and reflection."

Silla and Tyriqa walked together to the "Cabin of Courage" and settled into comfy leather chairs on opposite sides of the room. The window views were beautiful this time of day. The sunlight glimmered on the surface of the lake and the loons crooned.

Silla twirled a section of her hair as she started to journal to determine her goals for the next year.

1. I am going to "find my voice" and use it in my profession. Those men at my lab won't recognize me after this retreat.

2. To improve my communication and confidence skills, I'm going to take some classes on presentation and improv.

3. I will purchase Theodora's online course for building courage and confidence.

A few months after attending the retreat, Silla applied the skills she learned in her classes and began to speak up for herself and about her work. She even started to interject and offer other perspectives to the conversations. She gained respect as her voice was heard in the workplace. Within months, she found a cure for COVID-19 and is onto a cure for both cancer and Parkinson's disease. Silla also began a joint partnership with Tyriqa, tapping into her tech savviness to turbocharge awareness for both cures.

Tyriqa stared at the sunrise to provoke some thoughts about her future goals for the next year. She felt rejuvenated just thinking about the changes in her near future.

1. After perusing the web for open positions, she decided to stay with her current company.

2. She will apply for an internal sales role.

Within weeks of the retreat, Tyriqa had applied and been accepted for the internal sales role, and was happier than she ever had been. She won President's Club for two years in a row, and was asked to take a leadership role in the department. She couldn't be happier. It's the perfect blend of both of her favorite roles.

Elaine, Antonia, and Maalika walked together, engaged in excited conversation, curious about what goals they would set for themselves. As they entered the "Den of Decisions," they each picked different couches around the fireplace so they could be close to the warmth and snuggled into the comfy pillows on the couches.

Elaine wondered about her future. She decided that family was what was really burning a hole in her heart, and she would like to spend the majority of her time with them.

1. She embraced a lateral move at the same company in the part-time role of running the projects for nonprofits.

2. Elaine focused on her needs as a working mother.

3. She determined how she would utilize and prioritize her time at home with family.

4. She explored opportunities for career growth and future promotions.

5. Elaine looked forward to raising her children and growing her career alongside everything that is important to her.

Elaine's life was full and busy and glorious. She ran the household, spent time with the kids. Working had always fired up all of her cylinders, and she couldn't be happier. To stay focused and at the top of her game at work, she surrounded herself with allies, mentors, sponsors, and her supportive spouse. She knew she would need to invest in a coach soon, down the road, and began to prepare for that investment, knowing that her first choice was Theodora. Elaine also co-hosted a fundraiser with Maalika, as the retreat unearthed their common passion for giving back to their communities by paying it forward.

Antonia grabbed a blanket to put around her legs and feet. As she started to write down her goals, she smiled.

1. She already started the process to start her own full-service architectural firm in San Francisco.

2. She planned several trips to the Golden Gate Bridge each month; it called her by name and was one of her sources of inspiration that infused her with creativity.

As Antonia began to make a name for herself in "The City by the Bay," she had many large organizations approach her for installations. Corporations asked to sponsor her work and hired her to consult on art. She never hid the fact that she loves Wonder Woman, and she had several ultra-high net worth clients give her Wonder Woman mementos as thoughtful gifts. Word was out about her skill in metalwork because of the coin she created for the Alzheimer's Foundation. The producers of the next Wonder Woman movie commissioned her to design earrings for Wonder Woman in the movie. She went on to win awards for her design, and copies of the pair she made were exclusively carried by the high-end jeweler, Graff, for sale to the public at their global boutiques.

Maalika grabbed her water and took a long sip. This year was going to be big. She kept her plans a secret because so many people would be happily surprised.

1. Over Thanksgiving, Maalika proposed to Amanda while they were volunteering for Feeding America.

2. While she was on this retreat, Food Network called and offered her an opportunity to compete on a show with her famous dish.

3. Maalika added "write a cookbook" to her list of goals.

Maalika picked out the most delicate and robust shining diamond for Amanda. Also, as she loved Antonia's jewelry, she commissioned her to design the settings for Amanda's engagement and wedding rings. The final product was reminiscent of the styles Amanda had mentioned favoring over various shopping trips throughout the years. Amanda had no idea this was coming.

Three weeks after the retreat, Maalika prepared her chicken tikka masala on the Food Network's competition show and won! She loved the experience so much that, in addition to her daytime career, she launched a foundation for mental wellness as her philanthropic calling. In this plan for awareness, action, and appetite, she incorporated her love of cooking with all the foods that support optimum brain and immune system health. Wanting to give more back to her community, she wrote a cookbook as a fundraiser. It was a huge hit. She invited donors from all corners of the globe to send submissions to the cookbook and requested their help in raising money. The return of donations included contributions and collections made by some of the world's top chefs.

Full S.T.E.A.M. Ahead, indeed. Throughout our lives, professional and personal, challenges are thrown in front of us, and we face our own difficulties when we are called to step up. For each challenge we conquer, we build another layer of steel in our golden Wonder Woman wrist cuffs, compelling us to move forward and teaching us valuable lessons. For as long as we are grateful for the women who have steamrolled ahead of us to give us these opportunities; for as long as we fight for what's humanely decent, respectful, and life-giving and fulfill our own dreams; for as long as we continuously carve new opportunities and better work conditions for the generations that follow, we, together as women (while uplifting the supportive and innovative men in our lives), will always be moving Full S.T.E.A.M. Ahead.

RESOURCES FROM GAYLE

PILLAR 1 - Silla

BOOKS

- *From Tokyo with Love* by Sarah Kuhn
- *Ripping off the Hoodie* by Shannon Wilkinson
- *Slide:ology* by Nancy Duarte

PHILANTHROPY

- The Michael J. Fox Foundation | https://www.michaeljfox.org

WORKS CITED IN THIS CHAPTER

- Tech Jury | https://techjury.net/blog/women-in-technology-statistics/

PILLAR 2 - Tyriqa

BOOKS

- *Activate Your Money* by Janine Firpo
- *Strategize to Win* by Carla Harris

PHILANTHROPY

- Black Girls Code | https://wwwBlackGirlsCode.com
- Girls Who Code | https://www.GirlsWhoCode.com

PILLAR 3 - Elaine

BOOKS

- *How to Raise Successful People* by Esther Wojcicki

PHILANTHROPY

- American Heart Association | https://www.heart.org
- Mercy Home | https://donate.mercyhome.org

GAYLE'S PODCAST

Theodora Speaks™ | https://podcasts.apple.com/us/podcast/theodora-speaks/id1555760344

- S1:E08 - "One Good [Engineering] Woman" with Cheryl Maletich, Senior Vice President of Transmission and Substation at ComEd, a unit of Chicago-based Exelon Corporation (a Fortune 100 energy company)
- S2:E20 - "Encouraging Equality" with Alison McConnell, CMO of Publicis Health Media

PILLAR 4 - Antonia

BOOKS

- *The Leadership Renaissance: Blending the Art and Science of You in Five Simple Steps* by Teri Goudie, Dave Heilmann, Jim Hutchinson and Caylen Bufalino

PHILANTHROPY

- Alzheimer's Association | https://act.alz.org
- Susan G. Komen Foundation | https://www.komen.org

SUPPORT FOR SEXUAL HARRASMENT

Sexual Harassment Complaints: "How To Report Sexual Harassment At Work In A Step-By-Step Process" | lawkm.com

PERSONAL / PROFESSIONAL DEVELOPMENT

Codebreaker Technologies is the world leader in Personality Coding Technology with tools, training, and technology powered by B.A.N.K.® It is a scientifically validated methodology designed to predict buying behavior in nanoseconds.

I use the Codebreaker AI, their cutting-edge Artificial Intelligence, to analyze LinkedIn profiles, emails, websites, or any text to decode and speak to the person's (e.g. a colleague, friend, team member, client, customer) buying personality in nanoseconds.

You can take the personality assessment here. Typically, it only takes 90 seconds to complete:

https://www.mybankcode.com/TheodoraSpeaks

PILLAR 5 - Maalika

BOOKS

- *Burnout: The Secret to Unlocking the Stress Cycle*, by Emily Nagoski, PhD and Amelia Nagoski, DMA

PHILANTHROPY

- Feeding America | https://www.feedingamerica.org
- UNICEF | https://www.unicefusa.org
- United Way | https://www.unitedway.org

MENTAL HEALTH RESOURCES

- National Alliance on Mental Illness | https://www.NAMI.org
- Mayo Clinic | https://www.MayoClinic.com
- Web MD | https://www.WebMD.com
- Psychology Today | https://www.PsychologyToday.com/US to find a therapist in your area
- Substance Abuse & Mental Health Services Administration 24/365
  SAMHSA.gov | 1-800-622-4357
- Suicide Prevention Lifelines

  - **US National Suicide Lifeline 24/365**
    SuicidePreventionLifeline.org
    1-800-273-8255 / 911
    In English, Spanish, & For Deaf & Hard of Hearing

  - **International Suicide Prevention Lifelines**
    https://www.opencounseling.com/suicide-hotlines

Would You Like Gayle Keller to Speak to Your Organization?

Book Gayle Now!

Gayle accepts a limited number of keynote speaking / coaching / training engagements each year. To learn how you can bring her message to your organization, email Gayle@GayleKeller.org or visit https://www.GayleKeller.org.

Review Inquiry

Hey, it's Gayle here.

I hope you've enjoyed the book, and found it both useful and fun. I have a favor to ask you.

Would you consider giving it a rating wherever you bought the book? Online book stores are more likely to promote a book when they feel good about its content, and reader reviews are a great barometer for a book's quality.

So please go to the website of wherever you bought the book, search for my name and the book title, and leave a review. If able, perhaps consider adding a picture of you holding the book. That increases the likelihood your review will be accepted!

Many thanks in advance,

Gayle Keller

Will You Share the Love?

Get this book for a friend, associate, or family member!

If you have found this book valuable and know others who would find it useful, consider buying them a copy as a gift. Special bulk discounts are available if you would like your whole team or organization to benefit from reading this. Just contact Gayle@GayleKeller.org or visit https://www.GayleKeller.org.

ABOUT THE AUTHOR

Gayle Keller is an award-winning, seasoned technology executive with over 20 years' experience working in corporate America. As an executive, she experienced first-hand how women struggle to excel in the workplace, and how men struggle to understand and cohesively work together with women.

As a result, she launched her own firm, Gayle Keller LLC, to be a powerful leader, a positive role model to her two young girls, and a driving force in the revitalization of gender inclusivity in S.T.E.A.M. (Science, Technology, Engineering, Arts and Mathematics) industries.

She is hailed for her leadership, hands-on integrated programs, and her direct approach to shift the paradigm and culture of select companies and universities alike through her keynotes, presentations, advisory services, and coaching programs. Gayle also hosts a podcast series called Theodora Speaks in which she interviews "Theodoras" from all backgrounds who have taken the reins in their industries.

Gayle resides in the Midwest with her husband and two daughters.

Gayle can be reached at: https://www.GayleKeller.org